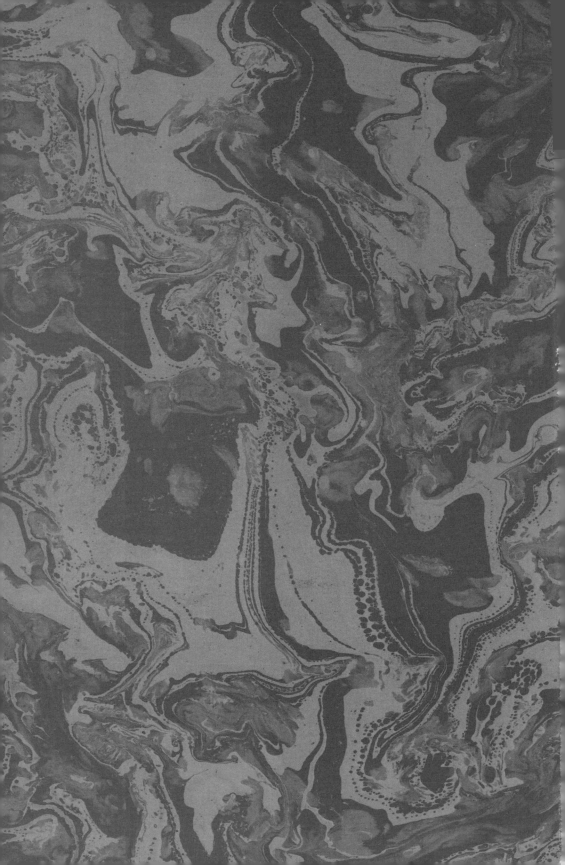

The Poems of
GOVERNOR THOMAS BURKE
of *North Carolina*

THE POEMS OF
Governor Thomas Burke
OF *NORTH CAROLINA*

On divers Matters, including a few written in Praiſe of the *American* War for Independence againſt *Great Britain;* & alſo a Number concerning a young Man's Affairs of the Heart.　　*　　*　　*　　*

Notice is hereby given that moſt of theſe Verſes have been tranſcrib'd from the original Manuſcripts & preſented for the firſt Time

To Which are affix'd an Introduction
　　　　　　　　& Notes by *Richard Walſer*

Publiſh'd to the World by the *State Department of Archives and Hiſtory* at the City of *Raleigh* in the State of *North Carolina.*　MCMLXI

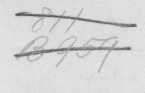

PS 721
B38
P6

STATE DEPARTMENT OF ARCHIVES
AND HISTORY

Printed in the *United States* of *America*
By *Judd & Detweiler. Inc., Washington, D. C.*

PREFACE

THE *State Department of Archives and Hiſtory* has publiſh'd many Volumes of documentary Materials, Finding Media, Pamphlets, and Leaflets, but it has never publiſh'd a Volume of Poems. Therefore, the *Department*, in publiſhing this Volume, in a Senſe, is departing from its uſual Policy. There is, however, a hiſtorical Baſis for ſuch a Departure. Many of the Poems reproduc'd here have never before been publiſh'd. Thus, they are original Material. Alſo, they were written by a GOVERNOR of the State.

Very few People realize that *Thomas Burke* (GOVERNOR, 1781-1782) wrote Poetry. Thoſe who are familiar with the State's Hiſtory during the *Revolutionary* Period know that he was a Doctor, a Lawyer, and a Public Figure intereſted in gaining Independence for the Colonies and particularly for *North Carolina*, but never knew he was a Poet.

All but Two of the twenty-three Poems exiſt in Manuſcript. Three of them are definitely known to have been publiſh'd in *Burke's* Lifetime, and Three Others after his Death. So far as can be determin'd, Seventeen are publiſh'd here for the firſt Time.

Richard Walſer, Profeſſor of *Engliſh* at *North Carolina State College*, decipher'd them from the original Manuſcripts, edited them, and wrote an Introduction and alſo explanatory Notes. The *Department* is glad to have the Service and Co-operation of *Profeſſor Walſer* in this Program. He is vitally intereſted in the Literary Hiſtory of the State and has done much to focus Attention on Literary Figures of *North Carolina* who otherwiſe would in general remain obſcure.

An Effort has been made to publiſh this Volume in a Format and Type Face of eighteenth-century Printing.

···{ v }···

The long "S," the diacritical Marks, Capitalization, Ligatures, and Italics uf'd in that Period have generally been follow'd. Alfo, an Effort has been made to procure Paper Stock and Binding fimilar to that uf'd in the Period.

D. L. CORBITT, *Head*
Divifion of Publications

Raleigh
April 16, 1961

CONTENTS

The Poems of
GOVERNOR THOMAS BURKE
of *North Carolina*

INTRODUCTION

THE dual Role of Literary Man and Man of Public Affairs is one of honorable Tradition in Hiſtory, reaching its moſt familiar Phaſe during the *Engliſh Renaiſſance* with such Names as *Sidney* and *Raleigh*. It croſſ'd the *Atlantic Ocean* with *Thomas Hariot* and *John Smith*, and by the Middle of the Eighteenth Century was everywhere evident among the educated Circles of the *Colonies*. In *Revolutionary* Times, there were Men like *Franklin* and *Paine* and *Waſhington* and *Jefferſon* who were expected to be Writers as well as Leaders. Poets were not miſſing among them, as the Careers of *Philip Freneau* and the various *Connecticut Wits* ſhow.

For *Thomas Burke*, the Role of Poet was far leſs pronounc'd than that of Man of Public Affairs. Yet Poet he was, and Poet he remain'd even after his firſt Acclaim as "Prodigy of Genius" had paſſ'd. Poetry, for *Burke*, was ſomething to cut his *Iriſh* Teeth on, ſomething to while away the Time with, ſomething in which he could give Expreſſion to his Moods, ſomething to enjoy. A Career as profeſſional Poet never enter'd his Mind; he was ſufficiently practical to realize that rough, young *America* had not reach'd, if it ever would, the Time when an Artiſt could be ſupported by his Art. Still, *Burke* gloried—for a While at leaſt—in his Poetry. Not till Domeſtic Preſſures and Public Duties crowded upon him did he neglect the *Muſe*, and even then he often reſum'd his Role as Verſe-Maker. Among his extant Papers are Lines written when he was hardly more than a Boy, as well as some compoſ'd at the Height of his Career, and at leaſt one carefully work'd out within a Year or two of his Death.

As literary Amateur, as Doctor and Lawyer, and as Man of State, *Thomas Burke* is repreſentative of thoſe many-talented Figures who founded our State and our Nation.

The short Life of *Thomas Burke*, whatever elfe one may fay, was certainly not dull. Like other Poets of the pre-Romantic Era, he was not of the retiring Sort, but took Part vigorously in the Events around him. Born about 1747 into a well-to-do Family of *County Galway* in *Ireland*, he grew up on the Eftate of *Tyaquin*, which had belong'd to the *Burkes* fince the Time of *Henry II*. He receiv'd a good Education. He knew *Latin* and *French*. Admitting that he learn'd eafily, he wrote that he had "acquired the art of methodizing [his] thoughts and rea-fonings." His Studies had oblig'd him, he declar'd, "to be much converfant in Books and Language."

At this Point, the Records are not clear. But about 1763, when he was only a Lad of Sixteen, he emigrated to *America*. Perhaps there were family Reverfes, or family Differences; it feems that he did not want to de-pend on the Bounty of certain Relatives. At any Rate, the Youngfter was plucky enough—as he was the Reft of his Life—to try fomething elfe when the old Conditions were no longer endurable. At *Accomack County* on the *Eaftern Shore* of *Virginia* he difcover'd a Haven and foon began the Study of Medicine. *Irishman* that he was, he quickly felt at home among the young Blades who rail'd at the Tyranny of *England*, actual or merely contriv'd. His natural Gifts and winning Perfonality alfo brought him into the beft Homes on the *Eaftern Shore*.

In Moments of Quietude, he wrote Poems—juft fuch Poems as a young Man would write. He fang his Hopes as a practicing Phyfician, he penn'd paftoral Lines on the Countryfide, and often he rhym'd his Admiration for the Ladies. The Writing of Poetry was a pleafant Avocation. For long, he faid, he had "lifp'd in Num-bers," but he had hidden the Propenfity, fearing the "Idle Character of a Rhimer." Practical *America* might think ill of a medical Man who fritter'd away his fpare Moments in flumb'rous Poefy. But the Urge to write was ftrong within him. He flung off his Stanzas in a private Shorthand which he had acquir'd. For a While, his fecret Sin was unknown.

It was during this Period that *Burke* met *Mifs Betfy Harmanfon*. The Letters he wrote her (whether the preferv'd Pages are the Originals unfent, or Copies, is uncertain) befpeak his Admiration for *Dean Swift*, for *Addifon's Spectator*, and for *Lady Mary Wortley Montague*. Concerning *Edmund Waller*, there was fpecial Mention. The proper young Lady, he advif'd, fhould perufe "the Works of Mr. Waller, a Poet who has always been the darling of the Fair & Judicious; long celebrated for the fmoothing of his Numbers Juftnefs and delicacy of Expreffion elegance & fprightlynefs of his Wit and tendernefs of his fubject . . . an author fo admirable for Eafy Harmony, artfull negligence, and a captivating variety of Subjects and Images." Already, *Waller's* rhym'd Couplets were ferving as Models for *Burke's* fecret Compofitions.

His letters of this Period are fill'd with Dicta on the Theory and Practice of Poetry. Its chief "End is to delight," he wrote, "and if the thing it avers be fact in the Mean it matters not how extravagantly it is painted, if you look into the Song of Solomon or even the Pfalms you will fee how extravagantly the one expreffes his refpect for the Deity and the other for his Miftrefs, from which we can only gather they were extravagantly pious and amorous. . . . Since I have got into Poetry and on a Subject naturally elaving [elevating?]," he continued, "fhall I, Mifs ———, prefume to ftrike with trembling Hand the Lyre, and with thy name awake the warbling Wire. In fhort I muft, for my pen will write no more profe, and you muft exercife your patience on what follows unlefs you are void of Curiofity which I by no means would have you be at prefent."

While we can affign no definite Poem as Appendage to this Letter to *Mifs Harmanfon*, we may be fure that if we could, it would be one *extravagantly amorous*, for *Burke* obferv'd that "nothing is more common than for every Song to make the bloom of the Beloved Surpafs every thing that can be Imagined, and the Lovers paffion to be capable of making him do even Impofibility, from all which we only expect the Poet thinks the Lady extremely Beautifull and that he loves her beyond what he is able to declare."

As to Technique in the writing and reading of Poetry, *Burke* advis'd: "First, as to rendering it, harmonious care should be taken to observe every pause and stop and the accent for the most part laid on every second silable—regard should be had for every note of admiration (!) or question(?)."

※ ※ ※

Thus, tho' the Medical Student practic'd his Art in Secrecy, he was nevertheless quite serious about it, and his conceal'd Propensity might never have been notic'd if, finally, his *Irish* Enthusiasm had not got the better of him.

In 1766, shortly after the glorious News reach'd *Virginia* in late *April* or early *May*, *Burke* wrote a Pæan on the *Repeal of the Stamp Act* at the Time when a Celebration was plann'd. This Poem, he said, "I shewed to one of my Intimates; being notwithstanding fully determin'd to conceal the author as much as might be, and give the Honor if any resulted from it, to him whom I design'd to speak it before the opening of the entertainment." Is there any Wonder that, in some magical Way, the real Name of the Author became known?

The Prologue was spoken, and *Burke* awoke to the Realization that he had become famous. This Effort of a "Single morning" got into Print, and "universal Approbation re-echoed from every corner."

Thenceforward, the Course of Poetry was straight ahead. For a While at least, he found himself (in his own Words) "at the head of the Literati of America, Esteemed the pattern of Taste and Prince of Genius." If we can forgive a young Fellow his Conceit in the Choice of Epithets when writing to the Family back Home in *Ireland*—for such was the Case—and for enlarging his Status beyond the Truth so that the Family would believe him a Success in a foreign Land where no parental Prop sustain'd him, we nevertheless have some Corroboration for his Words, even if less grandiose.

Once his *Repeal* Poem was abroad, once his Propensity was acknowledg'd, *Burke* sharpen'd his iambic Claws on the Issues of the Hour. Dismiss'd were the lovely Pastorals of *Accomack*, the dainty Words to the

Ladies. Stinging anonymous Rhymes of the Satirist erupted from the Pages of the *Virginia Gazette* in *Williamsburg*. If *Burke's* Contributions cannot now be nail'd down with any Certainty, the Authorship of his unsign'd Verses was at that Time fully recogniz'd when they appear'd. Again *Burke* was hail'd for his Genius. It matters not what the Issues were: when *Burke* participated in the poetic Battles royal in the Columns of the *Gazette*, he was the admitted Potentate. Unfortunately, there are more Poems *about* him than possible Poems *by* him in the surviving Numbers of the Paper. Only one Selection, indeed, can definitely be identified: his "Address to the Goddess Dulness" in the Issue of *October* 10, 1766, in which *Burke* gives the Cudgel to his Opponents.

On *November* 6, "Planter" was sorely upset at the literary Assassinations:

> Forbear ye wits your taunting wipes,
> Severe rebukes, indignant stripes;
> But chiefly thou the master, *Burke*,
> At tossing off poetic work. . . .

Burke's Blindness in one Eye was not overlook'd by the applauding "D. M." on *December* 18:

> *Burke's eye*, in double sense, is *single*,
> Enabling truth with wit to mingle. . . .

By *January* 1, an Opponent Satirist mention'd a Number of poetic and nonpoetic Contributors, then made Mention of

> The names of THESE (who reason brav'd,
> And high contempt) which BURKE engrav'd
> On two-fold FAME's black portal. . . .

A Week later, it was "poignant BURKE." On *January* 22, *Purdie's* ever-sprightly *Gazette* announc'd that the "exil'd Muse," banish'd from *Europe* in Shame for her Pregnancy, was being employ'd at "A———k" by "D———r B———." On the same day, *Rind's* rival *Gazette* down the village Streets of *Williamsburg* printed *Burke's* "Usurpation of Wit's Sceptre." While no Copy of *Rind's* Issue has been found, it was this Poem, along with the Poet's "Address to the Goddess Dulness," which call'd forth a nearly page-long Salutation in heroic Couplets titled "To the EAST, *A Replication from the Goddess* Dulness, To T. B., A Bard, of modern Note, *In the* EAST" by one who sign'd himself *Crambe*.   In angry Retort, *Crambe* noted that

> ravish'd Fancy, aiding Nature's Work
> Conceiv'd a one eyed Bard *ycleped* Burke. . .

and, after many roiling Lines, near'd his End with

> Now Burke adieu: your Laureat Task assume,
> To shine in Dulness for an Age to come:
> On ev'ry Subject, let your Metres fly;
> And live in Distichs, and in Distichs die. . .

then concluded

> Should Satyr ever pierce thee with its Pen,
> An *Epigram* will close the Wound again;
> If to your Front, your Fillet you apply;
> That Badge of true Hibernian Currency
> The Sat'rist must enrage; then damn at once,
> Each Line he writes, and *doubly dubb* him DUNCE.

At this Point, the battle Lines had obviously shifted, and the once rever'd *Burke* was now himself the favor'd *enfant gâté* of the Goddess.   Yet and still, even the lustiest Warfare can become wearisome, and already Officers and Soldiers with their verbal Cannon had begun to drift away.   A final Blast came in "The Metamorphosis" on *April* 9:

> O BURKE, to whom the flowing lines belong,
> Can you behold your patron suffer wrong! . . .

And then there was Soundlessness.

🙰   🙰   🙰

We can believe in the joyous Energy which the twenty-year-old Doctor put into poetiz'd Hostilities. If he sported a few shallow Wounds after this ridiculous *Armageddon*, there were Results realistic enough.   His Success in Affairs Political doubtless made him ponder whether or not he had chosen rightly in his Profession. A Lawyer was much more respected than a Doctor and, not only that, he got more Pay.   Ever ready for the

Untried, *Burke* turn'd to Law, tho' then and thereafter he was always fpoken of as *Doctor Burke*.

His Movements at this Juncture are wrapp'd in the Silence of the Unrecorded. He may have ftay'd in *Accomack County*, he may have mov'd up the River to *Richmond*, or he may have crofs'd *Chefapeake Bay* to ferve an Apprenticefhip in a Lawyer's Office at *Williamfburg*. Whatever his Peregrinations, two years later he was eftablifh'd as a Lawyer in the *Norfolk* area, where with undiminifh'd Brafhnefs he was challenging— actually challenging to a Duel—a Conteftant in a legal Matter.

For the Nonce, the fharp Vein of Poetry feems to have run out, efpecially after his unlucky Marriage in *March*, 1770, to the beautiful *Mary Freeman* of *Norfolk*. She was, from the firft (we learn from the Hiftorian), not "calculated to make his happinefs in domeftic life." She was neither fympathetic nor encouraging; Poetry would have bor'd her; there apparently was no middle Ground where their Differences could be refolv'd.

By 1771, bufinefs Fatigue and poor Health urg'd *Burke* to confider moving from *Norfolk*. Two hundred Miles to the Southweft, among the rolling Hills of *North Carolina*, lay the attractive village of *Hillfborough*, where, he wrote, the "Lands are fertile, the Water good, and the Climate remarkably moderate and healthy." In the following *March*, he was licenf'd to practice Law in *Orange County* there, and fome Months later fettled in the Vicinity. His Plantation was call'd *Tyaquin;* his Town Houfe, built after 1773, was later known as *Heartfeafe*. Soon after arriving in the Area of the *good Water*, the Lawyer, now working again but not fo ftrenuoufly, was once more in good Health.

As the Troubles with *England* intenfified, *Burke* fenf'd his old Vigor returning. His aggreffive Opinions and anti-*Britifh* Tendencies recall'd the vituperative Months of the *Virginia Gazette*, and the liberty-loving Folk of *Hillfborough* enjoin'd him to be their Reprefentative at *North Carolina's Second Provincial Congrefs*, to meet in *New Bern* on *April* 3, 1775, when there would be further Efforts to define the State's pofition in the Events of the Day. *Burke* alfo attended the *Third Provincial Congrefs* in *Hillsborough* on *August* 20, and the *Fourth* in *Halifax* on *April* 4, 1776. From the last *Congress* came the famous *Resolves* to actuate Independence from *England*.

The Poet in *Burke* must have been considerably repress'd by these Duties in the Public Service. The vigorous Republican was so elsewhere engag'd that the *Muse* had to absent herself for a while.

In *December*, 1776, *Burke* was elected along with *William Hooper* and *Joseph Hewes* to represent *North Carolina* at the *Continental Congress*. Beginning the next *February*, he spent the following four Years in and around *Philadelphia*. Within that Period, there were occasional Intermissions, of course, and a Number of Visits back to *North Carolina*. For instance, in *September*, 1777, he darted out of the City to serve as a volunteer Officer at the *Battle of Brandywine*. When the Nearness of the Enemy puls'd his fighting Blood, he could not sit calmly in the Halls of Deliberation. At *Brandywine*, he noted with Vexation what he consider'd the Inefficiency of GENERAL *Sullivan*, and after the *Battle*, pass'd Words with the defeated *American* Officer, then challeng'd him to a Duel. It seems that the Matter was fortunately patch'd up.

Burke's Irascibility was due, in great Measure, to his high Sense of personal Honor. If his Actions often made for difficult Situations, his self-evident high Principles generally led others to Forgiveness. But not always. One fam'd Story about him concerns the Time he retir'd from a lengthy Debate in the *Congress*, only to have a Messenger call for him to arise from his Bed and report to the Hall for a Vote. When he refus'd, saying he would not come for it was too late and too unreasonable, he was censur'd by the *Congress* after a fifteen-day Discussion of his Conduct, and a Reprimand of him was sent to his Constituents. *North Carolina* acted promptly: *She* sent him back to *Philadelphia* in spite of the *Congressional* Rebuff.

In the *Continental Congress*, his Position was usually that of an Independent, tho' he was strongly oppos'd to the *Articles of Confederation* and strongly in favor of State's Rights. Whatever his Leanings, he intensely and vehemently supported them. In the Affair of *Silas*

Deane, *Burke* re-invok'd his derifive *Mufe*, and the
Malevolence of his poetic Attack on ftaunch *Thomas
Paine* would have ruffled anyone but the granite Author
of *Common Senfe*. *Paine's* Actions, even tho' ill-advif'd,
hardly deferv'd the Contumely *Burke* heap'd upon him.
In an Enemy, one could expect *Burke's* Abufe and Hate.

If a Friend, one could expect his Love. Certainly,
the Ladies could reckon on the Affection of *Burke* the
Gallant. At firft, *Philadelphia* was a Holiday for him,
with its conftant Cotillions, delightful Affemblies, and
frequent intimate Gatherings where Ladies were clever
and beautiful. Even tho' *Mrs. Mary Burke* was often
in Town, her Hufband found Moments to pay his Re-
fpects to Intelligence and Lovelinefs. He wrote Poems
to and for the Ladies, and occafionally they replied in
Rhymes of their own. He fent them Letters, including
his Verfes, and hop'd they would underftand his Intention. Perhaps he wifh'd that they would fee in him a
"mifunderftood" Spoufe. On the Eve of the *Battle of
Brandywine*, it was *Chloë* (*Mifs Emlin*) who held his
Regard. Later there would be the "fair D——y" and
Delia. At the Boarding Houfe where he and *Cornelius
Harnett* ftay'd, it was *Mrs. Efther Vining* and her
Daughter *Mifs Vining* of marriageable Age. *Burke*
lov'd them all. The poetic Exchange between *Chloë*
and her *Colin* was well enough thought of to find a Place
in the Pages of the *Gentleman's Magazine*, one of the
moft influential *London* Periodicals of the Age.

The *Philadelphia* Years infpir'd *Burke's* lyric Pen to
an Intenfity reminifcent of thofe young Days on *Virginia's Eaftern Shore*. The exciting, cultural Life of the
City goaded *Clio* as well as *Erato*. Serious Hours in the
Congrefs were well match'd by elevated Evenings among
the Bright-Eyed and Quick-Witted. Yet, for *Burke*,
fterner Duties lay ahead and he became, finally, fome-
what wearied of the Huftle and Buftle, and very tir'd
indeed.

❦ ❦ ❦

In the Summer of 1780, he return'd to *Hillfborough*,
bufied himfelf with Army Supplies and *Tory* Foragers,
and for a while fat in the State *Houfe of Commons*. The
following Year he was back in *North Carolina* for good,

ſpending his Time in *Halifax*. Then, on *June* 25, 1781, tho' ſtill a Member of the *Continental Congreſs*, the radical *Thomas Burke* was elected GOVERNOR of the State by the *General Aſſembly* in a Conteſt with the conſervative *Samuel Johnſton*. *Burke's* immediate Problem was the Improvement of the *North Carolina* Troops, and for the next ſeveral Months he gave it his full Attention. Never far away, as he journey'd here and there, were the marauding *Tories*. They were cloſer than he knew.

On the foggy Morning of *September* 12, 1781, *Burke* was in *Hillſborough*, an inadequate Guard protecting him. Suddenly thro' the Miſt came a Band of the hateful *Tories*. The GOVERNOR of *North Carolina* was humiliatingly captur'd. As the Leaders *Fanning* and *McNeill* led their diſtinguiſh'd Priſoner towards *Wilmington*, they were in turn ſurpriſ'd by a Group of Patriots who, tho' ſpreading Havoc among the Royaliſts, were unable to ſet free the GOVERNOR. A Poetaſter deſcrib'd the Goings-On at *Hillſborough* and down Country in theſe limping Meters:

> The Governor and Council in Hillſborough ſought
> To eſtabliſh ſome new laws the Tories to ſtop.
> They thought themſelves ſafe and ſo went on with
> their ſhow,
> But the face of bold Fanning proved their
> overthrow.
> We took Governor Burke with a ſudden ſurpriſe,
> As he ſat on horſeback and juſt ready to ride.
> We took all their cannon and colors in town
> And formed our brave boys and marched out of
> town.
> But the rebels waylaid us and gave us a broadſide
> That cauſed our brave Colonel to lie dead on his
> ſide.
> The flower of our company was wounded full ſore.
> 'Twas Captain McNeill and two or three more.

In *Wilmington*, GOVERNOR *Burke* was impriſon'd, then later mov'd on to *Sullivan's Iſland* in *South Carolina* for ſafer Confinement. After *November* 6, when he was parol'd to *James Iſland* and put upon his Honor not to eſcape, he found himſelf in conſtant perſonal Danger from the wandering *Tories*. His Complaints to the

Authorities were ignor'd, and *Burke* reafon'd that the Terms of his Parole had been difregarded. On *January* 16, 1782, he fled the *Ifland* and two Weeks later, before an Exchange of Prifoners could be effected, refum'd the Governorfhip of *North Carolina*.

For this—the apparent Violation of his Parole—the GOVERNOR was roundly criticiz'd, for generally in *North Carolina* it was felt that *Burke* had been guilty of a difhonorable Action. Tho' he explain'd his Pofition in numerous Letters, even fuch an important Figure as *Nathanael Greene* had Doubts. To *Burke the Man of Honor*, this public Cenfure was inexplicable and un-bearable. His high Spirits droop'd as never before in his Life. Even Poetry, his Ally in Times paft, no longer fprang up jinni-like. In *Halifax*, at the requeft of young *Mifs Gilchrift*, he wrote a patriotic Poem on the Defeat of *Cornwallis* at *Yorktown*. As far as is known, it was his laft Offering to the *Mufe* who had ferv'd him well.

At the meeting of the *General Affembly* in *April*, 1782, *Burke* render'd a full Account of his Behavior, but when his Name was put in Nomination for Re-election, he declin'd to let it ftand. On *April* 23, *Alexander Martin* was chofen to fucceed him.

The fiery Patriot, his belov'd *America* free at laft but himfelf under a Cloud of Humiliation, attempted to take up again his Practice of Law. He thought of circum-venting his Shame—now mainly in his own Confcioufnefs rather than in the Minds of Others—by moving fouth to *Georgia*. He promif'd himfelf, at leaft, that never again would he enter into Public Life. And then, when an Illnefs came, he pufh'd himfelf ahead with his Work beyond his phyfical Powers. At Home, *Mrs. Burke* neither affuag'd his Wretchednefs nor comforted his Pain, and his lone Child, a Daughter, was too young to help. He died, ag'd Thirty-Six, at *Tyaquin* on *December* 2, 1783—in Self-Immolation on the Altar of his Honor.

❧ ❧ ❧

The Poetry of *Thomas Burke*, both Boy and Man, reflects the *Irifh* Volatility of a fentimental but forceful Perfonality. It is the Work of one who had faft Friends as well as invidious Enemies. Since *Burke* rarely wrote with Publication in Mind, Readers need not fear the Duplicity of the Poſeur or the calculated Artificiality of the would-be Profeſſional. In fact, his Verſe rings with the Sincerity of one whoſe Heart was ever on Diſplay.

He hated Sham, was quick in Reſentment, and ruſh'd into belligerent Defenſe of his Actions and Opinions. Tho' he once wrote an Eſſay againſt Duelling, at leaſt four Times in his Life he challeng'd thoſe with whom he was not in Agreement—the laſt Occaſion over the controverſial Breaking of his Parole. *Archibald Maclaine* predicted that *Burke's* Determination to "keep villains within their proper bounds and call ſcoundrels to a ſtrict account" would work politically "againſt his re-election" as GOVERNOR. And it did.

In ſpite of an impetuous Raſhneſs with its tragic Conſequences, *Burke* was ſo affable and earneſt, ſo frank and outgoing, ſo aggreſſively patriotic, and ſo ſolicitous of his Intimates that he was generally held high in Regard. His Verſe mirrors a convivial Story-Teller who could alſo hoiſt a merry Song. A *Catholic* ſtimulated in the Thinking of *American* Deiſm, he was a reſourceful Man happily at Eaſe in the Struggle for democratic Principles.

From a Look at the Titles in his ſmall but carefully choſen Library, one may apprehend the Drift of his Intellect and the partial Foundations of his Poetry. There were Law Books, of courſe, and curiouſly contraſting Treatiſes on Surveying and Midwifery. *Euclid* was preſent, and *Locke*, and Hiſtorians Ancient and Modern. *Cicero's Orations* and *Caesar's Commentaries* ſtood on the Shelf with *Vergil*, *Horace*, and *Terence*. A valued Copy of *Juvenal* taught him how to pour forth acrid Invective. In preparation for a Life as Doctor and Lawyer, Political Leader and Poet, *Burke* was well train'd by Books.

The beſt Poems of *Burke*, even when deficient in Imagery and repetitious in Vocabulary, are cogent and vivid Productions, ſure of Rhyme and Meter. Whether dainty Dedications to the Ladies or frenzied Slurs directed at his Opponents, they poſſeſs an effortleſs Attractiveneſs. What more noble Inventions might have fprung from him in a lefs ftirring Era, we do not know. We can be certain, tho', that they would have receiv'd the ftudied Workmanfhip characteriftic of the twenty-three Selections extant.

History has remember'd GOVERNOR *Thomas Burke* for the Groundwork he laid to protect the *Rights of the States* in the *Conftitution*. Hiftory has often recall'd his tragic End at the Dagger-Point of his Honor. It has term'd him one of the moft verfatile Men ever to hold Office in *North Carolina*. If Hiftory has neglected his modeft literary Attainments—the pleafant Occupation of an adroit Amateur—now for the firft Time *She* is humbly given the Opportunity of looking at this auxiliary Afpect of an amazingly well-rounded Eight-eenth-Century *Patriot* and GOVERNOR.

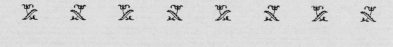

The Poems of
GOVERNOR THOMAS BURKE
of *North Carolina*

HYMN TO SPRING BY A
PHYSICIAN

MELODIOUS *Thomſon!* Fancy's darling Son!
Joy of the Nine! thy Muſes' Charms I own!
Forbear my Hand; in vain you ſweep the
Strings.
The Soul muſt feel, not ſpeak what *Thomſon* ſings,
Nor blind to Joys which blooming Nature yields:
The dew-ſtarr'd Verdure of the ſmiling Fields,
The budding Blooms that balmy Fragrance breathe,
The Foreſts twining with luxurious Wreath,
The joyous Pæans of the vocal Bow'r
Bliſs thro' my Boſom ſympathizing pour.
    Here did the Hand with cheerful Toil prepare
The fruitful Bleſſings of the bounteous Year;
Did cheerful Glades with rural Notes reſound
Heard from the Folds and furrow'd Plains around;
Here his own Flocks did ev'ry Shepherd feed;
Here did each Youth his own fat Oxen lead.
Great were my Joy to view the cheerful Swain
Force the bright Plowſhare thro' the reeking Plain,
To view the Seedman with his laboring Hand
Spread future Harveſt o'er the grateful Land.
    But here no Joys can *Ceres*' Labor yield
Since *Ethiop* Slaves deform the ſable Field!
Curſt be the Fiend who in our halcyon Clime
Sow'd the dire Seed of ſuch atrocious Crime!
O Liberty!
Yet Freedom here with brighteſt Verdure blooms:
No tyrant Hand the ſcorpion Rod aſſumes;
No haughty Lord with vaſt unwieldy Store
Treads on the Necks of the defenſeleſs Poor;
Each Swain of ample Competence poſſeſt
With peaceful Ease and rural Plenty bleſt.
Here, could Servility a Pleaſure find,
The Slave might bleſs the Lot by Heav'n aſſign'd;

Here mild Benevolence and Reaſon ſway,
And peaceful Servants their lov'd Lords obey.
    But when bright Pæans' mild aſſending Beam
Bids wide-ſpread *Cheſapeake* refulgent gleam,
Silent I muſe along th' extended Shore
And diſtant hear the hoarſe *Atlantic* roar.
To Nature's Wonders I expand my Eye,
And my Soul banquets on Philoſophy.
    Immortal *Newton* ſhows the Laws that guide
Bright Worlds unnumber'd thro' the boundleſs Void:
The wondrous Harmony of Nature's Laws
From ſelf-prov'd Facts to Demonſtration draws.
Unrival'd Man! what other ſhould I name?
What other Breaſt e'er held ſuch heav'nly Flame,
Emblazing Arts with Beams unknown before,
The Source and Current of each uſeful Lore?
    Nor thee, great *Locke!* while I admire the Mind
That could the Force of Heav'n's Effulgence find,
Can I forget, whoſe ſkillful Hand could trace
Our Underſtanding's no leſs wondrous Mace.
    Hail, heav'nly Minds whoſe Genius beſt can prove
The Soul immortal ſent from Realms above!
    Why ſhould I mention ev'ry precious Hour
With Joy devoted to Health's blooming Pow'r?
Spent with the Sages of *Hygeian* Lore,
To languid Cheeks who ſmiling Bloom reſtore?
O give me, *Phœbus!* all thy healing Art,
Teach me to baniſh Languor from the Heart,
To bid the Blood with gen'rous Vigor flow
And the calm Breaſt with conſcious Health to glow,
To fruſtrate each *Eumenidean* Bane
Tranſſuſing Bliſs for agonizing Pain.
    Or why the Time when I my Soul unbend
In Converſe gay with an ingenious Friend?
In *Tully's* Periods, or th' *Athenian's* Fire,
Alike *Calliope's* ſweet Voice admire?
Or hear delighted *Clio's* gorgeous Tale,
Or ſad *Melpomene* the Brave bewail?
Nor unobnoxious to the Flames that play
In ſweet *Thalia's* or *Erato's* Lay:
And oft our Souls indulge at Reaſon's Feaſt
While *Polyhymnia* ſpreads the rich Repaſt.

But far the greateſt of my Joys remain:
When the broad Sun converges to the Main,
Poſtpon'd each harſher Buſineſs of the Day,
I ſing exulting, to the Fair, my Way.
  Then ſprightly Mirth, gay Hopes, and ſoft Deſires
In my charm'd Breaſt awake Love's ſleeping Fires
While 'round the Board the beauteous Nymphs regale,
Where *China's* Gems the fragrant Balms exhale.
Gay Wit and roſy Smiles alternate grace
And ſpread freſh Beauties o'er each lovely Face.
  But ſtill moſt elegantly ſweet to Love
Are ev'ning Walks beneath the vernal Grove:
The ſmiling Maid makes Nature's Charms impart
New Bliſs, and wakes to livelier Joy the Heart.
The conſcious Soul in its Exiſtence bleſt
Exults with Tranſport in the bliſsful Breaſt.
Here does my Harp in vain attempt to dreſs
Each Angel fair with native Lovelineſs.
What Hand can paint each love-inſpiring Toaſt?
The ſhaded Banks of either *Hungars* boaſt?
Who ſhall each blooming *Harmanſon* rehearſe?
Who ſpeak a *Stith* in no unworthy Verſe?
Each lovely *Kendal*—what celeſtial String?
New blooming Charms of each *Eliza* ſing?
Fair Nymphs! ev'n now inſpiring ſoft Alarms,
Tho' ſcarce twelve Springs have open'd on your Charms!
Or heard or ſeen, alike reſiſtleſs found,
Or Wit or Mien inflicts the tender Wound.
  Theſe who would ſpeak, may paint the *Paphian*
    Court,
Or *Cynthia's* Partners in the rural Sport.
Oh! ſhould I join, how oft my Breaſt is torn?
What various Tumults in my Boſom burn?
What Pain, what Bliſs, what Tenderneſs, what Rage
Oft ev'ry Feeling of my Heart engage,
Relapſ'd to Love, tho' oft in vain decried,
When ſoft I languiſh by my Charmer's Side?
Reclin'd in fond Expectancy I lie
And catch each Glance in lov'd *Belinda's* Eye,
Or when ſhe ſtruggling yields the balmy Kiſs,
My Boſom melts with all a Lover's Bliſs.
  To thee, fair-blooming Spring, theſe Joys I owe;

Thy genial Warmth bids Juices livelier flow:
To Senſe more delicate each Fibre raiſe,
And Impulſe teach with nicer Touch to pleaſe.
Theſe, Spring beſtows and Liberty ſecures;
All Joy by thee, fair Liberty! endures:
Theſe, while a *George* fills happy *Britain's* Throne,
Spite of each Slave, each Tyrant, are my own.
One Subject happy in a godlike King
* * * * * * the joyful Spring!

LYRIC TO A LADY

ENCHANTING Maid, ſweet Empreſs of my
Breaſt,
The Seraph ſtands in all thy Air confeſt.
What God, invok'd, my Numbers ſhall inſpire
To ſpeak thy Beauties or my ſoft Deſire?
Thy Form's a Sun, and Beauty's ſplendid Rays
With boundleſs Force in Emanations blaze.
My Love—in vain—oh! read it in my Heart.
Let me, my Angel, all my Soul impart.
I'm all one Flame of Love— But hold my Hand!
In Time the Tumults of my Heart withſtand!
Hold, leſt the darling Theme too far engage
My trembling Strings in incoherent Rage.
But why, ſweet Nymph, ſhould I thy Name conceal,
Or rather aſk why ſhould the Muſe reveal
Who hears of Flow'rs but apprehends a Roſe,
Or who the Moon in full-orb'd Splendor ſhews?
Leſs Need my Love in airy Sounds be dreſſ'd
Known by ſuperior Splendor from the Reſt.

—*Carmina Muſæ contexent cunĉta Lepore.*

—*Obſcura de Re tam lucido pango.*

BENEVOLENCE

NOW while 'mongſt many leſs important Themes
Aloud each Voice Benevolence exclaims,
While Numbers plead this Virtue to excuſe,
Who ſacred Laws and truſted Pow'r abuſe,
Let me my Lyre invoke the tuneful Maid,
By whom the Souls in faireſt Light diſplay'd,
To paint this nobleſt Habit of the Breaſt
By which alone Humanity is bleſt,
By which alone ſubſiſts each social Tie,
By which alone we emulate the Sky.
　'Tis not Benevolence that bids Mankind
Be to groſs Follies and dire Vices blind,
That bids us melt with an unmanly Woe
When Villains writhe beneath Law's vengeful Blow.
'Tis not Benevolence that fondly draws
A Veil twixt Felons and avenging Laws,
That weeps the purple Murderer to ſee
In Gibbets parching on th' aërial Tree.
　When injur'd Juſtice lifts her angry Arm,
Benev'lence never will her Rage diſarm;
For only Juſtice can ſecurely bind
The equal Peace and bliſs of Humankind,
Reſtrain our Paſſions by the ſocial Seal,
And guard the private in the gen'ral Weal.
　See, while my Boſom boils with furious Ire,
My pale Lips quivver and my Eyes flaſh Fire,
My fault'ring Tongue and lab'ring Voice deny
Vent to my Fury in ſevere Reply.
Inſtant the murd'rous Dagger I arreſt
And point it raging at th' offending Breaſt.
　But ſoft!　I see the violated Laws
With doubling Vengeance vindicate his Cauſe.
Shall I then give to Infamy my Days,
By one mad Act my Anger to appeaſe?
What the dire Cauſe of ſuch tremend'rous Strife?

What mighty Wrong to be aton'd with Life?
  Perhaps he dar'd my Vanity or Pride
Kindly to check or gaily to deride.
For a kind Caution or facetious Word,
If in his Heart I plunge my thirſty Sword,
Meanly inſult him welt'ring on the Ground,
And loudly triumph in the deſp'rate Wound,
Is he to Virtue and Mankind a Friend
Who would th' Aſſaſſin from the Sword defend?

*   *   *   *   *   *   *   *   *   *
*   *   *   *   *   *   *   *   *   *

  Were Violence by Juſtice not reſtrain'd,
Soon ev'ry Hand would be with Murder ſtain'd.
Her ſable Flag dire Malice would diſplay
And wounded Nature ſicken at the Day.
Who views the Harlot's well-diſſembled Tears
When the ſoft Guiſe of tender Grief ſhe wears,
And feels a melting Influence impart
The Softneſs to his ſympathizing Heart
While tender Pity ſteals thro' ev'ry Senſe,
Then is it Weakneſs or Benevolence?
  Shall he who's dignified with public Truſt
For Virtue plead if he become unjuſt,
Squand'ring on Minions with profuſive Hand
Vaſt Sums extorted from a plunder'd Land,
What the poor Peaſant gains from labor'd Soil
By painful Vigilence and tedious Toil?
If he will Wealth to Fools and Pandars give
On which th' induſtrious Huſbandman ſhould live,
If he'll the Gameſter's craving Wants supply
Who riſks at once whole Manors on a Die,
If well-born Fools and Idlers he ſupport
In Splendor equal to the *Perſian* Court
Tho' not one Act of Goodneſs does adorn
Their Lives, or Virtue with their Souls was born—
Say, what Benevolence that could perſuade
To make his Country give ſuch Miſcreants Aid,
Give them the Labors of th' induſtrious Hind
Whoſe Weeds ſcarce guard him from the northern Wind?
  Not this which forced from my Breaſt the Sigh
When you, dear ——, with dejected Eye

Betray the Symptoms of a deep Chagrin
Or, ſoftly ſimp'ring, languiſh in the Spleen.
'Tis not—for then I feel my own Diſeaſe:
Unleſs you're happy, I forego all Eaſe.
Thy ſlighteſt Pang brings Anguiſh in Exceſs,
Yet Love, not Virtue, gives the ſoft Diſtreſs.
  But ſay, my Friend, for ſurely you can tell:
What is that Virtue you practice ſo well?
What is Benevolence, that Beam divine,
That muſt from Heav'n in Emanations ſhine?
'Tis that which bids the gen'rous Boſom glow,
Bids it with Love to Humankind o'erflow,
Feels as its own each virtuous Soul's Diſtreſs,
And burns to give all Nature Happineſs,
As that great Sun which in the Center burns,
Vaſt rolling Worlds illumines and adorns,
Holds Nature's Balance, emanates his Ray
Thro' Space immenſe, and Light and Heat convey.
So Virtue's Sun   *   *   *   *   *   *
*   *   reſt with   *   *   *   *   *   *
This, the great Source of their reflected Light
Glows in the Midſt with heav'nly Radiance bright;
Of all the Virtues the bleſt Source and Soul
Illumes, adorns, and animates the Whole.
Yet ſtill this gen'rous Friendſhip to Mankind
Is ne'er to Vice or poiſ'nous Folly blind.
The tender Meltings of a tim'rous Heart
Have not of Virtue the moſt ſhadowy Part.
  When *Jove* deſcends in gentle vernal Show'rs,
The Earth unbending ſpreads abundant Flow'rs,
All Nature's Face in bloomy Pride is gay,
And ſweet Profuſion ſcents the fragrant Day.
But when vaſt Torrents tumble from the Skies,
Beneath the Deluge Vegetation dies:
No Pride of Blooms, no gay enliv'ning Green,
But noiſome Weeds and dreary Waſtes are ſeen.
As fruitful Springs nor love much Drought or Rain,
So Virtue is twixt wide Extremes a Mean.
  That ſelfſame Breaſt which melts at tender Woe
Will with black Malice and dire Envy glow;
But that moſt happy, that moſt favor'd Breaſt
Which with ſerene Benevolence is bleſt,

Each weak Extreme perceives itſelf above,
Yet warmly glows with univerſal Love.
  Th' ALMIGHTY LORD of this ſtupendous Earth
Who ſpoke the boundleſs Univerſe to Birth
Thro' living Nature ſent benign his Voice:
"Love my Command, love Being, and rejoice!"
  O could the Muſe thy gen'rous Heart ſurvey,
Could ſhe thy Boſom to Mankind diſplay,
Inſtructed thence each Breaſt might learn to glow
For gen'ral Weal and what true Pity know.
There juſtly bounded ev'ry Eye might view
What Love, what Pity to Mankind is due.
Thence I Benevolence might juſtly draw
Where Virtue's govern'd by her own ſtrict Law.

A POET'S INSPIRATION

HAIL, graceful Spring, fair blooming Mildnefs'
    Smile!
    Pour thy gay Fragrance o'er the teeming
    Soil,
Wake the vaft Woods with Love's harmonious Sound,
And emanate thy genial Joys around!
While the glad Tenants of tranfparent Skies
At thy Approach bid warbling Raptures rife,
While the fweet Blooms Earth's verdant Surface drefs
And Nature feels what Nature can't exprefs,
My grateful Hand fhall touch the trembling Lyre,
My Voice fhall join the univerfal Choir,
I'll fing the Bleffings of my calm Recefs
And humble Blifs of rural Happinefs.
   Soon as *Aurora* from her purple Bed
Does the grey Dawn with fainter Blufh o'erfpread,
Rouf'd by the Matins of the plumy Throng
That ambient pour the wild harmonious Song,
Soon as my Sighs and plaintive Murmurs ceafe
For the dear Maid juft fnatch'd from my Embrace,
Raif'd from my Down, I bend my thoughtful Way
Thro' Groves, and meditate the tuneful Lay,
Great *Homer's* Genius, *Maro's* Art admire,
Or melting Softnefs of the *Lefbian* Lyre,
Or fometimes hear the *Teian's* warbling String
Refufe a Theme but genial Love to fing.
   On tender Myrtles and foft Herbage fpread,
While in his Arms his blufhing Fair is laid,
Sometimes his Brows with rofy Wreaths I twine,
While LOVE himfelf prefents his Bard with Wine:
Or oft the fportive *Sabines'* tuneful Page,
Peerlefs as *Pindar* in harmonious Rage:
Prince of the Lyre! I fee thy whirling Car
Borne by fwift Swans above *Olympian* Air:
The wond'ring Nations of the World fhall know
The Bard whofe Praife fhall Fame's own Voice outgrow.

Cana's fweet Voice oft warbles in my Ear,
Oft great *Fingal's* triumphant Arms I hear,
Majeftic *Offian*, thou whofe gen'rous Breaft
Was by *Apollo's* genuine Flame poffeft!
Great Rival of the loud *Mæonian* Lay!
Oft does my Breaft thy pow'rful Voice obey!
Melt with the Fair or emulate the Brave,
Or weep the Warrior in untimely Grave!

PASTORAL AT LECKLEIGH

HOW great the Joy to hymn our equal GOD
In Nature's Temple, the refounding Wood
Where with indulgent Love HIS bounteous Hand
With lavifh Beauty decks a fruitful Land!
Bleft Shades, how oft has been my vaft Delight
When fair *Aurora* fprinkled rofy Light,
Among your Glades to con the *Mantuan* Lay
Or with the tuneful *Teian* Lyre to play!
Beneath, while beauteous *Flora* fpreads her Charms—
Above, the Afh extends its fhady Arms,
Melodious Mufic breathing Charms around
And humid Pearl befpangling all the Ground.
    Forgive me, *Horace*, if the charming Voice
Infpir'd my Breaft with more ecftatic Joys
Than thy fweet Numbers, tho' thy tuneful Rage
Could charm my Heart and ev'ry Senfe engage.
    The thick'ning Hazels here a Plain inclofe
Where beauteous Flow'rs their modeft Bloom difclose.
A prattling Stream the flow'ry Earth divides
And with fomniferous, murmuring Mufic glides
Where, 'round, the fragrant Bow'rs to Love perfuade
And move foft Wifhes in the tender Maid.
While fhe beholds the flow'ry Couch beneath,
Th' embow'ring Shades foft Sighs fpontaneous breathe.
Inftant her Bosom with her Swain is fraught,
And her Soul melts at ev'ry tender Thought.
    Then, happy Flow'rs! in tender Ecftafies
The lovely Nymph, LOVE, meditating lies,
And fenfelefs Shades embrace thofe heav'nly Charms
Which Pride withholds from youthful *Strephon's* Arms.
For oh! 'tis Pride that flints the female Heart
And ftill invalidates the Lover's Art;
For tender Souls their angel Frames inform,
And genial Flames their melting Bofoms warm.

Ye virgin Fair, why do you then obey?
Why waſte the Sunſhine of your fleeting Day?
Her rougher Paths let colder Matrons tread:
But ſport, you Virgins, in Love's flow'ry Mead.
  Here once as muſing I reclin'd my Head,
Soft o'er my Limbs a balmy Slumber ſpread.
Straight to my View a lovely Nymph appears
That *Hebe's* Bloom and *Venus'* Beauty wears;
An Air divine informs each charming Grace
And a calm Smile o'erſpreads her angel Face.
Her nut-brown Hair adown her Shoulders flows
And fragrant Wreaths her beauteous Head incloſe;
The Roſes bloom between her riſing Breaſts;
A milk-white Zone her ſlender Waiſt inveſts.
In frequent Folds a ſnowy Robe deſcends
And 'round her Limbs in artful Volumes bends.
  "Hail, blooming Nymph! no doubt a heav'nly Maid,"
My raptur'd Tongue with trembling Accents ſaid,
"Doſt thou too love to ſport among theſe Bow'rs
And deck thy Forehead with their fragrant Flow'rs?
Doſt thou delight to hear this murmuring Stream
And here elude fierce *Sol's* meridian Beam?"
  "Profuſely ſweet the Spring ſo decks this place,"
The Nymph replied with ſweetly ſmiling Grace,
"That Gods with Joy forſake their native Sky
And on theſe Herbs in bliſsful Trances lie.
Idalia, Cyprus, or the *Paphian* Grove
Not ſo delight the beauteous Queen of Love
As does this Wood where *Cybele* beſtows
Each charming Sweet that from her Altar flows.
Her Joys here raviſh with more keen Delight,
For ſofteſt Love theſe ſmiling Shades invite,
As once the Pow'r with gay *Vertumnus* play'd
On tender *Lotos* in a *Cyprian* Shade.
  "The youthful God, while ſoft Senſation warms
Cloſely intwin'd by her fair folded Arms,
Thus ſpoke: 'Fair Queen, whom all the World adore,
Thou laughter-loving, ſweet-enchanting Pow'r,
Is there a Grove or ſhady Seat you prize
Above the Reſt that keep thee from the Skies?
Speak, and it always ſhall my Care employ
To make it ſtill inſpire delicious Joy

Unfelt before, the lov'lieſt Bloom diſplay
That decks the genial Boſom of the *May*.
Sweet od'rous Shrubs ſhall ſpring among the Trees
And *Flora's* faireſt Charms ſtill open to the Breeze.'
"He ſpoke, and thus the ſmiling Queen replied:
'Gentle *Vertumnus*, aye with youthful Pride
Bedeck'd, when Paſſion fires the tender Breaſt,
By gen'rous Deeds we ſpeak the Flame the beſt.
Great is the Bliſs for Lovers to beſtow,
But a much greater to our Loves to owe.
No fair Aſylum whither I retire,
Indulging Love or ſoothing ſoft Deſire,
So much delights me as my lov'd *Leckleigh*,
Whoſe pleaſing Bow'rs invite eternal Stay.
There, ſhould the *Titan* Band again aſſail
Olympus, would I all my Loves conceal.
There, there, *Vertumnus*, all thy Art employ
And if you can, more grateful Bloom ſupply,
More ſtately Trees, more Love's inviting Bow'rs,
More grateful Odors, or more beauteous Flow'rs.' "

YOUNG MAN'S THOUGHT

THE Queen who gives ſoft Wiſhes birth,
And *Bacchus*, God of Wine and Mirth—
Me, their Friend and Favorite, own;
And I was born for them alone.

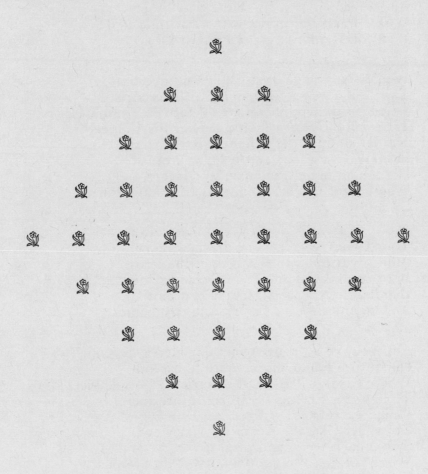

TRIUMPH AMERICA!

TRIUMPH *America!* Thy patriot Voice
Has made the Greateſt of Mankind rejoice:
Immortal *Pitt*, an ever glorious Name
Far, far unequall'd in the Rolls of Fame!
What Breaſt (for Virtue is by all approv'd
And Freedom ev'n by *Aſia's* Slaves belov'd),
What Breaſt but glows with Gratitude to Thee,
Boaſt of Mankind, great Prop of Liberty!

*   *   *   *   *   *   *   *   *   *

Would 'twere in Pity to Mankind decreed
That ſtill a *Pitt* ſhould to a *Pitt* ſucceed;
When proud Oppreſſion would ſubvert the Laws,
That ſtill a *Camden* ſhould defend the Cauſe.
Nor let's forget the gallant *Barré's* Merit,
His *Tully's* Periods and his *Cato's* Spirit,
His too an honeſt, independent Heart,
Where Fear nor Fraud nor Avarice have Part.

*   *   *   *   *   *   *   *   *   *

Proceed, great Names! your mighty Influence join,
Your Country's Arts and Policies refine,
Aſſiſt great *Conway* and reform the State,
Bid peaceful Commerce reaſſume her Seat,
Bid *Britiſh* Navies whiten ev'ry Coaſt
And *Britiſh* Freedom ev'ry Country boaſt.

*   *   *   *   *   *   *   *   *   *

And you, ye Fair, on whom our Hopes depend
Our future Fame and Empire to extend,
Whoſe fruitful Beds ſhall dauntleſs Myriads yield
To fight for Freedom in ſome future Field,
Reſign each Dear.   *   *   *   *   *   *
Today let Gladneſs beam in ev'ry Face,
Soften each Smile and brighten ev'ry Grace;
While the glad Roofs with lofty Notes reſound,
With Grace harmonious move the mazy Round;

Make our Hearts feel the long-forgotten Fire,
Wake into Flame each Spark of ſoft Deſire.
Too long indignant Tumults and Alarms
Have made us heedleſs of your lovely Charms.
But now beneath the downy Wings of Peace,
With Freedom bleſt, our Care ſhall be to pleaſe,
Each Day the genial Pleaſure to improve
And add new Sweetneſs to connubial Love.

ADDRESS
TO THE GODDESS DULNESS
From the Eaſt

Semper ego auditor tantum, numquamne reponam,
Vexatus totiens . . . .　　　　　　JUVENAL

HAIL Dulneſs, hail! thou cloud-compelling
　　Pow'r,
　　The Weſtern World thy riſing Reign adore.
　　What Crowds preſs forward to thy op'ning
　　　Fane!
What noble Pageants glitter in thy Train!
See Sages, Chiefs, the maſſy Altars raiſe!
See golden Vaſes heap'd with Incenſe blaze!
See Zeal, great Goddeſs, at thy dread Command
Fire ev'ry Heart and lift each armed Hand!
See, ſee each Quill, thy copious Influence ſhed!
See thy Fogs thick'ning 'round each drowſy Head!
Thy magic Miſts, involving ev'ry Eye,
The Earth envelop and o'erſpread the Sky.
　　See RIND and PURDIE, fluſh'd with Verſe and Proſe,
With rumbling Hum the reeling World repoſe!
See foaming BEN impel lethargic Lead
With equal Force from Cannon and from Head!
See unbred MANNERS, to advance thy Fame,
Boaſt with a Lie that *from the Eaſt he came!*
With matchleſs Impudence he pleads thy Cauſe,
Nor heeds or Virtue's nor his Country's Laws!
See deep PHILAUTOS, ethically grave,
Drench ev'ry Temple in the drowſy Wave!
Serenely dull! what Arguments proceed!
Such, Goddeſs, *Bavius* might with Rapture read!
　　Thou, too, METRIOTES, benign apply
Thy tickling, murmuring, ſoothing Lullaby;
Still *o'er* our Ears thy ſmooth, ſoft Periods roll
Till a calm Trance ylap each ſlumb'ring Soul;
O pour thy wond'rous Eloquence along,

As Cobwebs foft, as fubtle, and as ftrong!
He threats, great Goddefs! How he threats thy Foes!
His Champion BEN fhall pull the PROPHET's Nofe!
    Approach, great Days! Bleft Age of *Goths* and *Huns!*
For Law, give Cudgels! and for Wit, give Puns!
    See, from th' embow'ring Foreft's deep Recefs,
The *honeft* BUCKSKIN does thy Throne addrefs!
His marfhal'd Tropes and Metaphors he draws
To glorious Combat in thy much lov'd Caufe.
See, on his Writings the *hermetic Seal*
So firmly fix'd no Meaning can exhale!
Indulgent Goddefs! thy peculiar Care
This *hoary* General beft deferves to fhare.
Sacred to thee a Life of Toils he led,
From *acting active* thro' each Scene he fped.
In early Youth he dar'd that arduous Shore
Where thro' white Cliffs the hoarfe, rough Billows roar.
He fought thy Scholiaft with unwearied Pains
In *Thames'*, in *Cam's*, in *Ifis'* fair Demefnes.
Skill'd in each Art, at Length he quits the Strand,
A finifh'd Dunce to grace th' *Hefperian* Land.
    Hail Dulnefs, hail! again I greet thy Reign.
Such mighty Chiefs thy Empire fhall maintain,
Wit's fcatter'd Pow'rs fhall to *Bœotia* fly
And we for Dunces with *Batavia* vie.
    But ftill unfix'd, dread Goddefs, is thy Throne
Till BLAND, till LEE, till BOLLING are our own;
Till NICHOLAS' Eloquence and Virtue fail
With faithful Watch to guard the gen'ral Weal
While his firm Heart with gen'rous Pride difowns
Bafe Fear of Wrath and proud Ambition's Frowns;
While th' EASTERN BARD, in quaint prophetic Style,
Can force thy firmeft Partifans to fmile;
While with *Swift's* Humor, *Locke's* capacious Mind,
CAMM, thy worft Scourge, by Nature, is defign'd:
What fudden Horrors thro' my Bofom thrill!
O fhudder, Goddefs! fee, he takes his Quill!
The ready Off'ring from thy Shrine he tears
And bids Derifion feize thy Votaries' Pray'rs.
    Here all your Poppies, all your Rhymes at once
Pour down and make each hoftile Name a Dunce.
Thefe conquer'd, Wit fhall fink in one dead Calm,
And the whole Land enjoy thy foothing Balm.

FRAGMENT OF A SATIRIC POEM

*　　*　　*　　*　　*　　*　　*

ANOTHER Chief would think　　*　　*
Did not his Merit find　　*　　*
To pay a Share of what I owe,
This Favor on him I'll beſtow
And hope he'll take it in good Part,
As flowing from a grateful Heart:
Simpſon, I mean, who all his Life
Hath wag'd with Truth a mortal Strife,
The People's moſt obſequious Slave:
Juſt if they pleaſe; if not, a ———.
Who knows no Taſte of Good or Ill,
Except his Intereſt and their Will,

*　　*　　*　　*　　*　　*　　*　　*

On *Noyon's* Name ſo　　*　　*　　*
Nelſon the juſt, humane and kind,
With whom Diſtreſs is ſure to find
A lib'ral Hand, a gen'rous Mind,
Griefs, not his own, whoſe Boſom feels,
And where he can, their Miſery heals.
　Thus have I ſought, in artleſs Lays,
The Chief of Dulneſs' Sons to praiſe.
Tho' modeſt, they'll excuſe, I truſt,
Encomiums which are true and juſt

*　　*　　*　　*　　*　　*　　*　　*

*　　*　　*　　*　　*　　*　　or Fame,
*　　*　　*　　*　　*　　Life might blame,
*　　*　　*　　*　　*　　*　　them paſs,
And not do Juſtice to each Aſs;
The *Country Planter*, who exclaim'd
'Gainſt the Commiſſion, late ſo fam'd,
Who now his Head with Writing puzzles,

And now large Bowls of four Milk guzzles;[1]
The fenfelefs, blund'ring, ftinglefs Grub
Who fcrawl'd the firft and fecond Rub;[2]
With fome whofe Names I can't recall,
And fome who had no Names at all;
For, tho' the Querift *firft* began

* * * * * * * *
* * * * * * * *

In fpite of Knave or Fool or Afs.

MOROMASTIX

---

[1] Alludes to this Paffage in *The Country Planter:* "If we drink four Milk all the Week, we have furely a Right to the Butter on Sunday."
[2] Two Pieces call'd *The Scotch Rub*, written by one Revd *Cutler*, an illiterate Blackfmith.

TRANSMOGRIFICATION

UNWITTING, once *Actæon* ſtray'd
　To that ſequeſter'd Stream
Where, bathing, Night's reſplendent Maid
　Aſſuag'd the ſultry Beam.

More curious *Landon*, when the Queen
　Her Brother's Aid implor'd
And took Cathartics for the Spleen,
　Her ſecret Haunts explor'd

In Hopes the Off'rings *Cynthia* laid
　On *Cloacina's* Shrine
With Clinks and Rhymes might lend some Aid
　To eke his brainleſs Line.

Both guilty Chiefs her Vengeance ſhare;
　For ſtraight the prudiſh Laſs
Chang'd poor *Actæon* to a Deer
　And *Carter* to an Aſs.

Tho' by his Hounds *Actæon* bleeds,
　Yet *Landon's* Fates ſurpaſs him:
Since none annuls another's Deeds,
　No God can e'er un-aſs him.

QUATRAIN

WHAT Voice thus grows upon the Wings of
         Fame?
    Sonorous, lofty, ſtrong and clear?
    Sure, *Bland* or *Phœbus* calls upon my Name
And pours full Tranſport on th' admiring Ear.

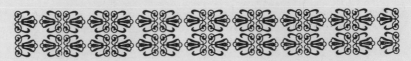

ON SEEING AN EXTRACT
FROM THE BOSTON CHRONICLE

ILLUSTRIOUS Fair! be yours the Pride to warm
  Thofe Hearts whom Virtue and true Glory charm

*   *   *   *   *   Sentiments admir'd
*   *   *   *   *   *   *   *   *   *

For whilft, heroic Nymphs, infpir'd by you,
We fight, no Force our Carnage can fubdue.
Your Virtues add new Vigor to our Arms;
Ev'n Freedom gains new Value from your Charms.
While nobly confcious that for both we fight,
Ev'n Wounds on Wounds and Toils on Toils delight.
At length our   *   with *   *   *   *   *

*   *   *   *   *   *   *   *   *   *

COLIN AND CHLOË

To *Chloë*

YOU aſk me, fair *Chloë*, to ſtrike the gay Lyre,
　　Once more to attempt the ſoft Strain:
Alas! long neglected has ſlept ev'ry Wire,
　　And I ſtrive to attune them in vain.

The Time is no more when a Virgin's bright Eyes
　　And ſweet Smiles could gay Tranſport impart;
No more from fair Bloom thoſe Emotions ariſe
　　Which once ſo enchanted my Heart.

While Freedom and Peace bleſt each ſylvan Retreat
　　And ſecur'd ev'ry Bliſs to the Swain,
How jocund the Woodlands my Song did repeat
　　While Beauty inſpir'd the ſoft Strain!

Now tyrant Ambition extends his dire Arm
　　And threats our free Land to enſlave:
No Muſic is heard but the Drum's hoarſe Alarm,
　　No Song but the Dirge of the Brave.

No more ſoft Emotions become the firm Breaſt;
　　To theſe, fiercer Paſſions ſucceed:
Indignation for Rapine and Beauty diſtreſſ'd,
　　And Vengeance for Brothers who bleed.

Theſe ſtretch out each Arm to graſp the long Lance,
　　Theſe fill ev'ry Boſom with Rage,
Theſe impel even Shepherds in Arms to advance,
　　Theſe, theſe ev'ry Soul muſt engage.

In vain, then, fair *Chloë*, my Hand would eſſay
　　To awake to ſoft Concord the Lyre;
Each String vibrates War, ev'ry Sound bids away,
　　Theſe Times other Efforts require.

Even *Chloë's* ſweet Smiles unſucceſſful muſt prove,
　　Even her gentle Accents muſt fail:
My Boſom alike denies Muſic and Love
　　Till our Arms o'er our Tyrants prevail.

But Freedom and Peace to our Land once reſtor'd,
    Thy Commands, lovely Nymph, I'll obey;
My hand ſhall with Pleaſure forego the dread Sword
    And my Lyre ſhall reſound the ſoft Lay.

Chloë's Reply to Colin

Sly Reynard *eſpied a Crow light on a Spray*
    With a Prize that he wiſh'd to poſſeſs;
Complimenting to gain it, he judg'd the beſt Way
    And thus did the weak one addreſs:

"Thou Goddeſs of Melody, prithee beſtow
    One Lay to divert a true Friend."
By Vanity blinded, the ignorant Crow
    With her Diſcord the Æther did rend.

Should I, like the Bird, ſweet Harmony court
    'Gainſt Nature, ſhould court her in vain,
Contemn'd by Good-Senſe, and of Satire the Sport,
    Reflection would follow with Pain.

But ſince Colin's *late Favor claims my Reveries,*
    Tho' Prudence enjoins to deſiſt,
Mild Gratitude bids me endeavor to pleaſe,
    And his ſimple young Friend will perſiſt.

Does lordly Ambition wage War in our Land?
    If ſo, of that Dæmon beware;
Nor let fiercer Reſentment your Counſels command,
    Leſt the Fate of old Satan *you ſhare.*

But as Friends and Protectors of Virtue and Truth,
    Prove theſe to your Meaſures gave Birth;
And the World ſhall confeſs you, in Age and in Youth,
    Delegated by Heaven and Earth.

Let the Blood of the Harmleſs for Vengeance ne'er cry,
    Leſt ye taſte of thoſe Bitters ye ſend;
For that POWER SUPERIOR, *on whom they rely,*
    The Guiltleſs will ever befriend.

In Time both your Strength and Exertions may fail;
    And reduc'd to the utmoſt Diſtreſs,
Your fervent Petitions to Heav'n may prevail,
    Tho' your earthly ones met no Succeſs.

By conqu'ring, we *should* not Tranquillity find,
    As Paine *doth delusively say.*
'Tis the Conquest of Vice and Corruptions of Mind
    That must hasten the glorious Day.

When her Banner a permanent Peace shall here raise,
    When Swords shall to Plowshares give place,
Not barely Profession, but CHRIST in our Ways,
    Must the Horrors of Discord erase.

Did the Horse know his Strength, he would quickly be free,
    And did Man the high Pow'rs of his Mind,
They would nobly forgive and gain true Liberty,
    As future bright Ages shall find.

Come, Colin, acknowledge this Doctrine is right,
    The Test of true Patience and Worth,
That 'tis highly unlawful for Christians to fight
    Or the Shiloh was ne'er upon Earth.

May the Warriors of every Nation agree
    And Love universal abound!
Were their Bosoms from Passions disgraceful but free,
    Sweet Concord would soon spread around.

Simplicity then shall erect her Domain,
    Whose peaceful and innocent Smiles,
Captivating the Hearts of each Nymph and each Swain,
    Put the Serpent to flight with his Wiles.

If too freely I've caution'd, and spoke what occurr'd,
    Good-Nature, I hope, will excuse:
Remember, 'twas Colin's *Request* that incurr'd
    What Chloë must blush to peruse.

Colin to *Chloë*

Had the Bird whom you sing, gentle *Chloë*, possess'd
    A Voice so harmonious as thine,
Each Savage, relenting, of Rage 'twould divest,
    And each Fraud make the Cunning resign.

Belov'd of sweet Harmony! think not in vain
    Your Vows to her Shrine you address:
'Tis she tunes the Numbers of *Chloë's* sweet Strain,
    And her own gentle Soul you possess.

My lovely young Friend! no Endeavor to pleaſe
    A Soul ſo refin'd can require;
Simplicity, Elegance, Sweetneſs, and Eaſe
    Like thine, all who ſee muſt admire.

What Prudence enjoins to ſuppreſs the ſweet Lay
    Whoſe Precepts the Boſom improve,
Whoſe gentle Perſuaſions each Heart muſt obey,
    While at once they both charm and reprove?

Sweet Moraliſt! ſtill be thy Precepts divine
    To *Colin* thus ſweetly convey'd;
His Reaſon preſumptuous, well pleaſ'd, he'll reſign,
    Nor queſtion the Truths they perſuade.

That Virtue and Innocence, Freedom and Peace
    Make all the true Bliſs of Mankind,
That Wrongs to forgive is the *Chriſtian's* true Praiſe
    Thy Song has deep-fix'd in his Mind.

With thine will he join his benevolent Pray'r
    That Warriors their Rage may forego,
That Love univerſal and Virtue may ſhare
    O'er Man all Dominion below.

How can you too freely your Cautions expreſs?
    Or what ſhall Good-Nature excuſe?
Why bluſh, lovely Nymph, at thy Song of mild Peace
    Which Angels well-pleaſ'd might peruſe?

Tho' *Colin's* rough Numbers Indulgence require,
    Tho' rude and diſcordant his Lay,
How great is their Merit, ſince *Chloë's* ſweet Lyre
    They moved ſo divinely to play.

Chloë to Colin

So kindly invited, how can I refuſe
    To proceed on a Theme ſo ſublime,
Tho' unpractiſ'd in Verſe and unfit to amuſe
    With the flowery Strains of good Rhyme?

And has the bleſt Doctrine which Chloë *has taught*
    Impreſſ'd the gay Mind of her Friend?
A Creed that, with Clemency, Purity fraught,
    Points out a deſirable End.

Or has the soft Dictates Politeness conveys
    Forbid what she says to oppose,
And the Forfeit Sincerity fled from his Lays
    That to dwell with Deceit never chose?

No! rather suppose Colin wisely concludes
    That Truth can with Truth never jar,
From a Seat in his Bosom false Reas'ning excludes,
    Fit only to sport at the Bar.

"As your heavenly FATHER is perfect, be ye"
    Is our SAVIOR's most gracious Command;
Renounce brutal Nature and like Angels be,
    Since this Effort HE's pleas'd to demand.

How enobling to Man is that Virtue divine
    That "reviles not again, when revil'd"!
In this heavenly Duty, how much would he shine,
    Exalted, endeared, and mild,

That views with Forgiveness a Brother's misdeeds,
    Bids Malice and Hate to depart,
For his Errors in Conduct compassionate bleeds
    With benevolent Feelings of Heart!

The Reverse is that Character, martial and fierce,
    That ne'er quells but increases his Ire—
That can stretch out the Lance Fellow-Beings to pierce
    And with Rapture behold them expire—

That with impious Ardor encounters in fight
    And, with Thirst of Revenge unallay'd,
Lays prostrate his Victims with savage Delight
    And gluts o'er the Havoc he's made.

If enough of poetical Fire I possess'd,
    I would melt with my Picture of Woe;
Of the Orphan's Complaint and the Widow distress'd,
    Most plaintive my Numbers should flow.

If aught should arise that would tend to sweet Peace,
    Embrace the dear Ensign of Joy,
Nor let an inflexible Temper increase
    Lest your Credit should meet an Alloy.

Feel the Pulfe of the People, their Echo remain,
    Leſt their Fury ſhould turn upon you.
But ſtop, darling Girl! nor preſume in this Strain
    To preſcribe to a BURKE what to do.

RUTHLESS WAR

WHEN gentle *Chloë's* fweetly pleafing Strains
    Her meek Religion's awful Truths impart
Of ruthlefs War, when her fweet Voice complains,
    In vain would Reafon guard the yielding Heart.

Colin, too, feels his injur'd Country's Woe;
    He deeply mourns the Wound at which fhe bleeds,
To his fair Friend would give at leaft to know
    From Force, not Choice, we join the deathful Deeds.

That heav'nly Temper, which forgives all Wrongs,
    Thofe Errors weeps in which a Brother ftrays;
Alas! fair Nymph, to few too few belongs;
    Revenge and Rapine mark our joylefs Days.

Ambition proud and Avarice fevere
    Invade our Land acrofs th' *Atlantic* Main.
Nor ours the Crime that lifts the pointed Spear
    Amidft his Fields to pierce the peaceful Swain;

Not ours the Crime that bids the weeping Maid
    The ruffian Soldier's brutal Rage deplore;
No Hofts of ours a kindred Race invade
    And fpread wide Wafte along their diftant Shore.

No Crime of ours involves the Winter's Skies
    In Smoke from Towns to hoftile Flames confign'd,
While Regions 'round return the doleful Cries
    Of Babes that welter to the freezing Wind!

Not ours the Crime that calls a favage Race
    From diftant Wilds the murd'rous Knife to fpeed;
To fpread relentlefs, unreftrain'd Diftrefs
    Alike where Hufbands, Wives, and Infants bleed.

Peaceful our Ports receiv'd *Britannia's* Ware
    And rich Returns each ebbing Tide convey'd;
Peaceful we toil'd along the ruftic Year,
    All harmlefs fcatter'd thro' primeval Shade.

Say then, fair *Chloë!* can celeſtial Pow'r
   Bid us our Breaſts to hoſtile Swords reſign?
Can *HE* whoſe Goodneſs Earth and Heav'n adore,
   This blameleſs Race to tyrant Rage conſign?

Is it *HIS* Will that howling Bands in Arms
   Should tear the Conſort from her Huſband's Bed?
Should ſeize our Virgins, fair in blooming Charms,
   With hands from Blood of ſlaughter'd Sins ſtill red?

Our future Race for haughty Lords ſhould toil?
   For Lords whoſe Rapine no Reſtraint ſhall know
For ruthleſs Tyrants till this fruitful Soil
   Where firſt our Labors taught the Grain to grow?

Does *HE* command that this deſtroying War
   Rage unreſiſted o'er our waſted Plains?
Sends *HE* this fierce, remorſeleſs Race from far
   On our free Necks to fix a Tyrant's Chains?

Look 'round, fair *Chloë!*   See that gracious *HAND*
   On ev'ry Creature, Art or Force beſtow,
And hear great Nature's awful Voice command
   Each to reſiſt or circumvent his Foe.

Shall Man alone, that favor'd Child of Heav'n,
   As of Mankind the mildeſt and the beſt,
To whom are Courage, Force, and Wiſdom giv'n,
   To ſlaught'ring Swords reſign the paſſive Breaſt?

Shall we our Wives, our Maids, our Infants yield?
   Our Fields made fertile by paternal Toil?
Or ſhall their Arms our patriot Warriors wield
   And guard our Country from relentleſs Spoil?

Had Heav'n, my *Chloë*, will'd to Human Kind
   A Life from Wrong, and vengeful Paſſions free,
Heav'n would have given to each thy gentle Mind,
   And each made gen'rous and refin'd as thee.

Then fierce Deſire for others' Rights unknown,
   No Wrongs or Rage would urge Mankind to Arms:
The peaceful Breaſt no other Warmth ſhould own
   But the mild Flame inſpir'd by Beauty's Charms.

To this foft Pow'r each willing, vanquifh'd Swain
    Would, unrefifting, yield his happy Breaft:
And thou, fair Nymph, fhouldft fpread thy gentle Reign
    And thy foft Sway by half Mankind be bleft.

Let us meantime benevolent deplore
    Neceffity that kindles fierce Alarms,
Weep ev'n the Wounds wherewith our Foes we gore
    Tho' awful Juftice confecrates our Arms.

Altho' his Arm the patriot Sword fhould wield
    And with juft Vengeance tho' his Breaft fhould glow,
Colin's rude Soul fhall to thy Numbers yield
    And learn to pity ev'n a wafting Foe.

Nor farther urge, fweet Moralift, thy Pow'r
    Than from Excefs to ftop the righteous Ire,
Still to mild Clemency his Breaft reftore
    By the foft Charms of thy melodious Lyre.

AN EPISTLE

HAIL, mighty *Thomas!* in whofe Works are feen
A mangled *Morris* and diftorted *Deane;*
Whofe fplendid Periods flafh for *Lee's*
  Defenfe,
Replete with ev'ry Thing but *Common Senfe.*
You by whofe Labors no Man e'er was wifer;
You of Invective, great Monopolizer;
You who, unfeeling as a *Jew* or *Turk,*
Attack a *Jay,* a *Paca,* and a *Burke;*
You who in Fervor of fatiric Vein
Maul and abufe the mild and meek *Duane,*
And eager to traduce the worthieft Men
Defpite the Energy of *Drayton's* Pen!
 O fay, what Name fhall dignify the Lays
Which now I confecrate to fing thy Praife?
In Pity tell, by what exalted Name
Thou wouldft be damn'd to an eternal Fame?
Shall *Common Senfe* or *Comus* greet thine Ear?
A piddling Poet or puff'd Pamphleteer?
Behold, around thee, how thy Triumphs lie,
Of Reputation's Hofts before thee die!
 On Envy's Altars, Hecatombs expire,
And *Faction* fondly lights *her* Pupil's Fire—
That Pupil moft devoted to *her* Will,
Who for the Worthlefs wags his quibbling Quill,
And with a true Democracy of Spirit
Bravely attacks the moft exalted Merit.
Thou Pupil worthy *her* attentive Care,
By *Satan* granted to *her* earneft Pray'r!
 When on the Brink of Fate fmooth *Adams* ftood
And faw his *Arthur* flound'ring in the Flood,
While plaufive *Richard,* in whofe gloomy Breaft
Revenge and Terror ftood by Turns confeff'd,
Doubtful his Brother's Meafures to defend,
With *Berkenhout* their Confidant and Friend,
Or, breaking thro' the weak fraternal Ties

To fave himfelf, the Doctor facrifice—
'Twas in that defp'rate, that important Hour,
When *Faction*, trembling for *her* tott'ring Pow'r,
Thus pour'd *her* Vows:
                              "Author of ev'ry Crime!
Whofe Pangs fhall laft beyond the Reach of Time!
By all thofe Crimes and all thofe Pangs, give Ear!
And if, O Sire, *thy Daughter* e'er was dear,
If e'er obedient to *her* Father's Call,
The Crowds of *Faction* fill'd his fpacious Hall,
If e'er the Populace by *her* poffeff'd
Have plung'd their Daggers in a patriot Breaft
And forc'd Humanity herfelf to fly
With banifh'd Juftice to yon azure Sky,
Attend, attend, attend, *my* Fav'rites fee!
Their hopelefs Eyes are fix'd alone on thee.
O help them, fave them, or *my* Sway is o'er,
Oppreff'd like thee, like thee to rife no more."
    The Pray'r was heard; the dreadful Monarch fpoke
While *Hell*, convulf'd, e'en to her Center fhook:
"Since on Mankind to fix my iron Reign
Nor Sin nor Death fuffice, I give them *Paine!*"
    Say, mighty *Thomas*, on what awful Day
You firft beheld the Morn's refplendent Ray?
That Day to Envy fhall moft facred be
And all her quinting Sons fhall wait on thee.
    But fure, no mortal Mother did thee bear;
Rather a Colic in the *Prince of Air*,
On dufky Pinions borne o'er Æther's Plain,
Expell'd thee from him with a griping Pain.
For as *Minerva*, Queen of Senfe Uncommon,
Ow'd not her Birth to Goddefs or to Woman
But foftly crept from out her Father's Skull
At a fmall Crack in 't, when the Moon was full—
So you, great *Common Senfe*, did furely come
From out the Crack in grizzly *Pluto's* Bum.
    Such as thy Origin, fuch be thy Fate,
To war 'gainft Virtue with a deadly Hate;
By daily Slanders earn thy daily Food,
Exalt the Wicked and deprefs the Good,
And having fpent a lengthy Life in Evil,
Return again unto thy parent Devil.

TO MRS. VINING

ON HIS DEPARTURE FROM PHILADELPHIA
AUGUST, 1779

MADAM, farewell, at length the Hour is come
Once more that calls me to my ruſtic Home;
That Hour much wiſh'd for, and much
   dreaded too,
Points to ſweet Home, but bids me part from you,
Begins my Courſe to meet domeſtic Friends
But here with you my happy Converſe ends.
   No more, returning from the Stateſman's Toils,
At thy kind Accents and benignant Smiles
The jarring Tumults of my Breaſt ſhall ceaſe
And to mild gen'rous Sympathies give Place;
No more I join thy Griefs for Wretches' Woes,
Thy Joy when Heav'n on Virtue Bliſs beſtows,
Admire thy patient, gentle, gen'rous Mind,
Quick to each Senſe, yet piouſly reſign'd,
Wit mild and bright like Ev'ning's parting Ray,
Manners refin'd, ſoft, affable and gay.
   Such oft have taught me to forget my Smart
And pour'd ſweet peaceful Pleaſure o'er my Heart.
Such now I leave! Such ſhould with Grief reſign;
Tho' all in Proſpect, Paradise were mine;
Such ſhall in pleaſing, ſad Remembrance keep
Till Death ſhall wrap me in eternal Sleep.
   Yet ere I go, I will indulge one Pray'r,
Altho' ſuch Goodneſs be Heav'n's darling Care;
Nor can my humble, wretched Mind preſume
By Pray'r to change the univerſal Doom;
Yet will I breathe this Pray'r to eaſe my Breaſt:
"Long may you live in all your Wiſhes bleſt,
For ne'er did Wiſh within that Boſom glow
But ſuch as Angels might with Pleaſure know;
And may no Length of Time or Space prevail
Of me Remembrance from thy Breaſt to ſteal;
May you ſtill know me what I wiſh to be
Far as my Pow'r can reach—a Friend to thee."

LOVE OF GLORY

WHILE fair *D——y*, *Maitland*, o'er thine
    Urn
Wakes her fad Lute in fweeteft Strains to
    mourn—
If Love of Glory did thy Breaft infpire
And, after Death, furvives the Soul's Defire—
Thy Shade fhall triumph, fince the Fair One's Lays
Embalm thy Name with everlafting Praife!
In Camps, in Senates, tho' thy Worth were known,
Tho' many Laurels by thy Sword were won,
Her Tear, alone, fhall make thofe Laurels bloom
Still with frefh Pride around the Warrior's Tomb.
Her tuneful Sigh fhall waft thy favor'd Name
From Age to Age with bright immortal Fame.
    But know, fair Mourner, ftill untaught to *fear*,
Untaught to *bend* by any hoftile Spear,
That Foe who could, in adverfe Ranks, admire
And praife the Breaft that glows with gen'rous *Fire*—
Tho' flow receding from the well-fought Field,
Their Force repulf'd—their Courage ne'er could yield.
Firm, but not *haughty*, to their Ranks return'd,
Each Hero's Bofom with frefh Ardor burn'd,
There wait the Fight.
               And, tho' by *Maitland* led,
The *Britifh* Foe within their Forts recede
Safe in thofe Works his Skill had taught to grow,
Juft 'fcap'd from Conqueft by as brave a Foe,
Wifely refolv'd no more to urge their Fate
Againft thofe Arms whofe Force they felt fo late.

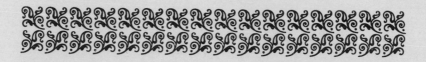

A NEW SONG

I know that Fair whofe lovely Mien
Still gay, ftill foftly mild is feen,
Whofe Words with gentle Sweetnefs roll,
Whofe Song enchants the raptur'd Soul,

Whofe Humor free, whofe Wit refin'd,
Whofe Senfe unconfcious charms the Mind,
Whofe gen'rous Pity mourns each Woe,
Each Pain the wretched Breaft can know.

I know this Fair. 'Tis her whofe Charms
Once fill'd each Youth with foft Alarms,
For whom the veteran Hero figh'd—
—'Tis gallant *Strephon's* blooming Bride!

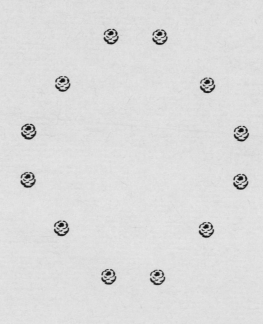

A LOCK OF DELIA'S HAIR

THRICE happy Hand! who late thro' Life ſhall wear
A ſacred Lock of charming *Delia's* Hair—
Wreath'd into Emblems of her heav'nly Mind—
Tho' mild, yet gay; tho' tender, yet refin'd—
Nor ſtol'n, nor raviſh'd from her beauteous Head,
But given, all bounteous, by the gen'rous Maid,
A Pledge of Friendſhip, tender and ſincere,
Such as an Angel might to Mortals bear.

Such Flames, alone, can in her Boſom glow,
Nor can my Breaſt a ſofter Paſſion know.
Too late for Love: that youthful, wayward Gueſt
With Hopes and Fears no more diſturbs my Reſt.
Long ſince, for me, his Art and Pow'r have ſped
And crown'd my Wiſhes in the nuptial Bed.

Her graceful Elegance and blooming Charms
Bid each young Heart beat high with Love's Alarms;
But milder Warmth her gentle Smiles inſpire
In Breaſts that feel no more his wild Deſire:
Affections mild, reſpectful and benign,
Friendſhip improv'd to Tenderneſs divine
Without the Tumults of th' impaſſion'd Soul
When Youth's Luxuriance ſtoops not to control.

This Lock ſhall witneſs that fair *Delia* knows
Such Flame benign in *Damon's* Boſom glows:
While twin'd, faſt by, his ſilver Hair ſhall prove
The Gift, the Pledge of Friendſhip, not of Love.

PENSIVE DELIA

DELIA is penfive! Mourn, each lovely Grace:
Your faireft Fav'rite yields to foft Diftrefs!
Let not one Smile the female Face adorn!
Let ev'ry Youth with keeneft Anguifh mourn!
Like mine, let ev'ry Bofom yield to Grief,
Nor, till fhe fmiles, or hope or wifh Relief!
But, O kind *Venus*, if on Earth thy Sway
Deferves thy Care, once more make *Delia* gay!
Her penfive Brow fufpends all foft Defire;
The Soul's gay Tranfport her fweet Smiles infpire.
O Queen of Charms! the dire Chagrin remove!
Reftore her Smiles and all the World fhall love!
Wit, Senfe, and Beauty fhall once more engage
Youth's glowing Breaft, the fond kind Wifh of Age;
And charming *Delia* fhall at length confefs
Her Smiles tranfport us, and her Griefs diftrefs.

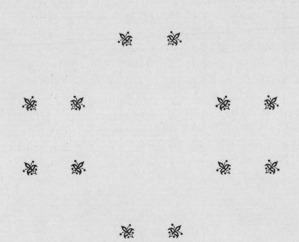

TO UNRESPONSIVE DELIA

YOU bid me, *Delia*, tune the moral Lay,
Nor let one Love-Note thro' the Numbers
play;
Hard is the Talk at thy Command to ling
And check the Warblings of each lofter String.
While o'er thy Charms enchanted Fancy roves,
The Heart to none but tender Impulfe moves;
Still, tun'd in Concord with the Heart, the Lyre
Yields Sounds refponlive from each trembling Wire.
   No Mufe, on me, the happy Verfe beftows
That, fmooth and tuneful, on each Subject flows.
Unfkill'd with Reafoning to convince the Mind
Or with fmooth Periods charm the Tafte refin'd,
Scarcely can I in humble Profe unfold
The plain, dry Tale where fimple Facts are told.
And only then can my rude Voice effay
The lofty Rhyme or fofter *Sapphic* Lay
When my Breaft feels a Tranfport from the Theme
Or melts to Love's or Friendfhip's tender Flame.
   Then afk not, Fair One, what the Fates withftand,
What Nature gives not to this artlefs Hand.
As foon the Flute could like the Clarion found
And call fhrill Echoes from the Vales around,
As could thy *Damon* to the Verfe impart
One Thought that fprings not from the melting Heart.
Forever filent muft the Lyre remain
Unlefs it anfwers to the heartfelt Strain.

DAMON'S ADVICE TO HIMSELF

DAMON, no more, thy fond officious Care
Employ to pleaſe the cold, reluctant Fair;
Conceal'd Impatience and Diſdain ſuppreſſ'd
Too well declare how you affect her Breaſt.
  Let others, free and happy, near her ſit,
Enjoy her Smiles, admire her ſparkling Wit,
Behold her Mien relax'd to tender Eaſe
And each kind Look confeſs how much they pleaſe.
  Aloof be thou, nor others' Bliſs deſtroy;
That Pleaſure mar not which you can't enjoy;
Fly, nor once more give lovely *Delia* Pain;
No more compel her to ſuppreſs Diſdain.
Be gen'rous thou, nor ever more impart
Unkind Emotions to a tender Heart:
That Heart, ſoft Inmate of the lovelieſt Frame,
Warm'd by each mild, each pure, each gen'rous Flame.

SONG FOR MISS GILCHRIST

LET Bards who give Voice to the Clarion of Fame
The Worth of our Chiefs and our Soldiers proclaim.
Such, only, can *Washington's* Glory pursue:
Too sublime for our Notes and too bright for our View.

Let them paint our Forces, with *France's* conjoin'd,
Display'd before *York*, and *Cornwallis Burgoyn'd*.
Bid Ocean, asserted, triumphant display
The Navy that freed her from *Britain's* proud Sway.

But let softer Scenes which we hope to enjoy
Henceforth, gentle Fair Ones, our Voices employ;
Our Husbands, our Lovers restor'd to our Eyes
Our Cheeks know no Tears, and our Bosoms no Sighs.

No more shall the dread Apprehensions affright,
Of Soldiers by Day and Assassins by Night;
Serene, bright and cheerful, our Days shall now prove
And our Nights know no Tumults but Transports of Love.

To make Home delightful henceforth be our Care,
With delicate Skill the rich Feast to prepare,
To converse with Variety, Spirit and Ease,
And with elegant Novelty always to please,

When Mothers, to rear the young Heroes to Fame
And infuse the true Sparks of the future bright Flame,
To deck the young Virgins with Graces refin'd,
And embellish with Sense and good Humor the Mind.

NOTES

In the Office of any important Eighteenth-Century Printer was an influential Perfon call'd the *Corrector*. It was his Duty to emend and "correct" the Copy before and after it was fet in Print. Confequently, the Author paid little Attention to Mechanics of Styling, and moft of the Conventions which are apparent in the Documents of the Era emanated from the Habits and Partialities of the *Corrector*. To a great Extent, the Author depended on him to fhape the Material into acceptable Form.

In tranfcribing *Burke's* Poems for this Book, the Editor has attempted to fill the Role of the *Corrector*. Truthfully it would ill ferve a Reader to have inflicted upon him *Burke's* Spellings and Capitalizations and Punctuation — efpecially his Punctuation, erratic and irregular even within one Poem. The *Corrector* has not, however, dar'd to change *Burke's* Words. Except in obvious Cafes where *Burke* or his Printer flipp'd momentarily, the *Corrector* has feen to it that the Poet's Phrafing is untouch'd.

The Styling of the prefent Edition is generally that of the mid 1700's, when there were generous Capitalizations particularly of Nouns, and frequent Italics for proper Names and important Words. Thro'out, in fhort, the Poems have been regulariz'd in order that they may be prefented uniformly, not as Oddments of verbatim Tranfcriptions difficult to read. This Styling has been follow'd alfo, except for quoted Matter, in the Editor's Introduction and Notes.

Of the many Sources confulted by the Editor, only a few need be lifted: Burke Papers, State Department of Archives and Hiftory, Raleigh; Burke Papers, Southern Hiftorical Collection, Univerfity of North Carolina Library, Chapel Hill; Purdie's and Rind's *Virginia Gazette; The State Records of North Carolina* (1895-1914); J. D. de Roulhac Hamilton, "Governor Thomas Burke," *North Carolina Booklet*, VI (October, 1906); Jennings B. Sanders, "Thomas Burke in the Continental Congrefs," *North Carolina Hiftorical Review*, IX (January, 1932); Elifha P. Douglafs, "Thomas Burke, Difillufioned Democrat," *North Carolina Hiftorical Review*, XXVI (April, 1949); Edmund C. Burnett, ed., *Letters of Members of the Continental Congrefs* (1921-1931); Ralph T. Whitelaw, *Virginia's Eaftern Shore, a Hiftory of Northampton and Accomack Counties* (1951); Sifter Mary Carmelita Barrett, "Thomas Burke, Governor of North Carolina" (Catholic Univerfity of America thefis, 1946); and Ruth Franklin Sutton, "Thomas Burke" (Univerfity of North Carolina thefis, 1949).

Concerning the Poems, all but Two of the Twenty-Three exift in Manufcript. Only Three of the Total are definitely known to have been printed in *Burke's* Lifetime, and Three others after his Death. Seventeen, as far as can be determin'd, are here printed for the firft Time.

The Twenty-Three by no means reprefent the Whole of *Burke's* Work. The *Virginia Gazette (Williamfburg)* has many Poems which eafily could be from *Burke's* Pen: "On the Death of the Hon. John Robinfon, Efq.," in *Rind's VG, May* 16, 1766; "Amacita and Lachrymæ," in *Purdie's VG, September* 5, 1766; "Canzonet," in

Purdie, October 17, 1766; "To Mifs E. B.," fign'd *Strephon,* in *Purdie, June* 2, 1768; and a whole Series fign'd *Caledonienfis,* in *Purdie, September* 15, 1768, to *March* 16, 1769. All have *Burke's* favorite Rhymes and Allufions. Yet fo much Eighteenth-Century Poetry was fimilar and derivative that to claim thefe Selections for him without certain Proof would be recklefs. Poets of the Time almoft never fign'd their Names to their printed Compofitions. One can believe that the highly productive *Burke* has many anonymous Stanzas hopeleffly hidden away in the contemporary Prefs, not only in the *Gazette* but elfewhere.

A half Dozen or fo of *Burke's* Poems could unqueftionably be added to the prefent Twenty-Three if the metrical Lines he wrote in Shorthand (manufcript Pages in the *Burke Papers, State Department of Archives and Hiftory, Raleigh*) could be decipher'd. Alfo, the now miffing *January* 22, 1767, Iffue of *Rind's Virginia Gazette* printed his "Ufurpation of Wit's Sceptre," which on *March* 12 *"Crambe"* defcrib'd in fome Detail. The Poem was faid to have contain'd *Burke's* "rhapfodic Scrap on himfelf" from a "Manufcript Edition" circulated under the Title "Rhapfodies of the Eaft." Then, finally and regrettably, a pofthumous Poem, faid to be in the *North Carolina Journal (Halifax)* in *September,* 1795, cannot be found in any of the Iffues for feveral Years before or after that Date.

Frequently, Writers on *Burke* have noted that fome Twenty-Two of his manufcript Poems are preferv'd in the *State Department of Archives and Hiftory.* The actual count is Nineteen, of which feveral are only Fragments. The Error is forgivable, fince a Number of the Poems are made up of feemingly unconnected Pages. Furthermore, Three of the Manufcripts, at leaft Two of them in *Burke's* Handwriting, are fimply not his Work. "The Petition of the Fools to Jupiter: A Fable, Suppofed to be Written by David Garrick, Efq., to Lord Chefterfield," evidently copied by *Burke* because he admir'd it, has right-hand Margins fill'd by him with Verfes in his Shorthand. The "Prologue to *No Man's Enemy but His Own,*" with a reverfe-fide Notation that it was "Spoken in Philadelphia in the winter of 1777," cannot be *Burke's.* This Comedy by *Arthur Murphy* under its correct Title *No One's Enemy but His Own* was given at the *Southwark Theater* in *Philadelphia* on *January* 19, 1778, by *Britifh* Officers, Soldiers, and Wives then occupying the City under *Sir William Howe.* Scarcely would an *American* Patriot at that Date be delivering a Prologue in a Theater under *Britifh* Aufpices. More than that, the "Prologue" is decidedly unlike *Burke's* other Pieces. Perhaps he copied it with the Intention of ufing it as a Model for Prologues of his own. A third Poem in the *Burke Papers,* "The Lamentation of a Sow, on a late *Annual Thankfgiving Day,* at Danbury in Connecticut, among that order of Diffenters, who emphatically call themfelves Saints," is, according to *Burke's* Notation, "By J——F——n" (*John Filfon?*) It is a lively Satire, but not in *Burke's* creative Vein.

Tho' few of *Burke's* Lines are conclufively dated, the Poems have prefently been arrang'd in what is their general chronological Sequence. For the undated Pieces, *Burke's* Handwriting, his Style, and particularly fome Internal Evidence place them in the Period of his Life in which they were written.

❧ ❧ ❧

HYMN TO SPRING BY A PHYSICIAN (page 17) is untitled in the two manufcript Fragments in the *State Department of Archives and Hiftory.* The laft Line is mutilated beyond the Poffibility of a reafonably accurate Tranfcription.

This is an early Poem written during *Burke's* fojourn in *Accomack County, Virginia.* Certainly his Acknowledgments that "a *George* fills happy *Britain's*

Throne" and that he himfelf is a "Subject happy in a godlike King" would prove that he was not yet indignant over the *Stamp Act*. Other Evidence of its early Compofition is its Diffufenefs, its youthful Diforder. Names from Mythology, *English* Philofophy, and thofe of perfonal Acquaintances range haphazardly thro'out the Piece. Near the Beginning, *Burke* decries Slavery, yet fenfes no Violation of Mood when he concludes with a love Paffage. It is the only Poem in which he mentions his Life as a Doctor.

James Thomson, nam'd in the Invocation, is the fam'd *Scotch* bucolic Poet. The practical Philosophy of *Sir Ifaac Newton* and *John Locke* appeal'd to *Burke's* deiftic Inclinations. In the Context of the Poem, *Phœbus* is the *Father of Medicine; Æfculapius* was *Phœbus'* Son. *Eumenidean* connotes *avenging*. After a Reference to *Cicero* and the *Athenian* (probably *Demofthenes*), *Burke* calls on only Six of the nine Mufes.

Hungars names a Creek as well as other geographical Spots in *Northampton County* on the *Chefapeake Bay* Side of *Virginia's Eaftern Shore. Harmanson, Stith,* and *Kendal* are, according to *Burke's* following Line, young Girls "fcarce twelve" years old. During the Eighteenth Century, all three Surnames were well known in *Northampton County*, juft fouth of *Accomack County*, where *Burke* had settled. Elfewhere it was "the Lovelinefs of Mifs Harmanfon" which fet *Burke* aglow. He addreff'd her varioufly as "Mifs Betfey" and "Mifs B.," commending her for rejecting her Suitors. She was ftill, he infifted, quite young. "I confider you," he wrote her, "as one of the moft brilliant Diamonds capable of the moft Exquifite polifh. Nothing could give me greater pleafure than to affift in the polifhing of so ineftimable a Jewel." At another Time, after penning some innocent Comments, *Burke* burft forth: "I have madam a ftrong temptation to enter upon a more tender Subject, but fear of giving Offenfe prevents me." By 1791 *Betfey Harmanfon* was married to a man nam'd *Wilkins*, her Sifter *Sukey* to a *John W. Kendall.*

The *Paphian* Court pertains to *Paphos*, City in *Cyprus* where a Temple was devoted to the Goddefs of Love.

LYRIC TO A LADY (page 21) is piec'd together from two untitled manufcript Sheets in the *State Department of Archives and Hiftory*. Proof of its early Compofition is that its firft eleven Lines occupy the fame Sheet as the clofing Paffage of "Hymn to Spring by a Phyfician."

In fpite of an expected Artificiality, no careful Reader will doubt that, in this Poem at leaft, *Burke* was in a rapturous Paffion ("I'm all one Flame of Love —"). Could the Lady be *Mifs Betfey Harmanfon?*

The Firft of the two *Latin* Epigrams, badly fpell'd in the Manufcript, may be tranflated "With Charm the Mufes weave together their Songs"; the Second, "From obfcure Matter I compofe the very clear." Their Originality is doubtful.

BENEVOLENCE (page 22) feems fairly complete in the three untitled manufcript Segments at the *State Department of Archives and Hiftory*. Mutilation is refponfible for the Lofs of at leaft two whole Lines and a Number of Words in two others. Both Style and Handwriting indicate an early Compofition.

Burke's Argument, addreff'd to a Lady who has defended Benevolence as a Doctrine, is that it muft never prevail over Juftice and true Virtue. At that Time such a deiftic Point of View was, of courfe, altogether anti-privilege, unfentimental, and *American*.

A POET'S INSPIRATION (page 26) is match'd from two untitled manuſcript Pages in the *State Department of Archives and Hiſtory*. Among the Claſſical Words, *Maro* is a Reference to *Virgil*, *Teian* to *Anacreon*, and *Sabines* to the original *Latins*. Apparently *Cana* is a ſhorten'd Form of *Canace*, Daughter of *Æolus*. Since *Mæonia* is the traditional Birthplace of *Homer*, the Adjective *Mæonian* is ſynonymous with *Homeric*. *Fingal* and *Oſſian*, ancient *Gælic* Heroes, were populariz'd in the Poetry of the *Engliſh* writer *James Macpherſon*.

PASTORAL AT LECKLEIGH (page 28) is aſſembled from two untitled Manuſcripts in the *State Department of Archives and Hiſtory*. Stock Device in the Hiſtory of *Engliſh* Verſe is the *Dream*, in which a Nymph or Goddeſs ſpeaks to the Poet. *Leckleigh* was obviouſly a Country Seat viſited by *Burke*. One can eaſily believe that the Poem was written as a Compliment to his Hoſt. In ſpite of Repetitions, this is one of *Burke's* happieſt Efforts.

Only a few of the claſſical Alluſions need Explanation. *Mantuan* refers to *Anacreon*. *Idalia*, *Cyprus*, and the *Paphian* Grove were favorite Haunts of *Venus*. *Cybele* was the Goddeſs of Nature, *Vertumnus* the God of the Seaſons. *Strephon* is a poetic Name for a Shepherd. *Lotos* is an old Word for Lotus-Eaters.

YOUNG MAN'S THOUGHT (page 31) is from an untitled Manuſcript in the *State Department of Archives and Hiſtory*. It was written on the Back of a Letter. The Handwriting indicates an early Compoſition.

TRIUMPH AMERICA! (page 32) is from an undated manuſcript Letter to *Burke's* Uncle in *Ireland*, preſerv'd in the *Southern Hiſtorical Collection*. Errors of the printed Verſion in the *State Records of North Carolina*, XIX, 921-926, have been corrected. Afteriſks deſignate a Tear in one Place of the Manuſcript.

The four brief Excerpts are from a much longer, now loſt Poem written on the *Repeal of the Stamp Act* in 1766 when *Burke* was only nineteen. Much of the Background of its Compoſition is related in the Introduction to this Book. News of the *Repeal* reach'd the *Coloniſts* about the Firſt of *May*. For an Entertainment celebrating the *Repeal*, according to the Letter he wrote his Uncle, *Burke* compoſ'd in one Morning "a prologue" which was enthuſiaſtically receiv'd by the Audience and ſoon was "in print." (The printed Copy has not been located.) Thereafter, *Burke* wrote, he "was look'd upon as a Prodigy of Genius."

Burke extols *William Pitt*, *America's* Champion in the *Houſe of Commons*, and alſo the *Earl of Chatham*, who argued in the *Houſe of Lords* that *Parliament* had no Right to tax the *Coloniſts*. *Iſaac Barré*, whom *Burke* compares to *Cicero* (*Tully*) and *Cato*, was *Pitt's* oratorical Ally in *Commons*. It was *Henry Seymour Conway* who mov'd the *Repeal* in *February*, 1766, and won a Majority. In the ſecond Segment, *Burke* is quite prophetic. Tho' no future *Camden* came to defend the *American* Cauſe, a younger *Pitt* did indeed ſucceed to an elder one.

ADDRESS TO THE GODDESS DULNESS (page 34) was printed in *Purdie's Virginia Gazette* on *October* 10, 1766, where it was titled merely "From the East." It is the only one of *Burke's* Poems in the *Gazette* to be identified without Reservation. In *Rind's Gazette* of *March* 12, 1767, "*Crambe*," in his Poem to *Burke*, three Times mentions the "Eaſtern Bard's Addreſs to the Goddeſs Dulneſs" and makes Alluſions to various Paſſages in it.

For Months, *Burke* had follow'd the involv'd Squabbles, domeſtic as well as political, which had fill'd the *Gazette* Columns from the Offices of both *Purdie* and *Rind*, who were publiſhing Newſpapers with an identical Title. With a few Exceptions *Burke* here condemns all the pſeudononymous Belligerents, referring Admiration near the End of his Piece for only a Few of his Heroes. Even an extended Treatment of the Times would hardly suffice to clear up the local Embroilments; moreover, it would be unneceſſary. *Burke's* Strictures of thoſe whoſe Writings he deſpiſ'd as dull involve the Perſons themſelves, not the Iſſues.

The *Latin* Motto introducing the Poem is the opening Line and a Half of *Juvenal's Firſt Satire:* "Muſt I always be only a Liſtener? Never reply? I who have been bor'd ſo often?" Thus *Burke* announces that his Couplets will ſcourge the Fools of Dulneſs in the Tradition of the *Latin* Satiriſts and the ſharp-tongu'd *Engliſh* Poets like *Dryden* and *Pope*.

BEN, MANNERS (whom *Burke* reſented because of his pretending to come, like *Burke* himſelf, *from the Eaſt*), PHILAUTOS, METRIOTES, and BUCKSKIN were Pen Names of *Gazette* Correſpondents — all of them, according to *Burke*, Adherents of the Goddeſs. *Bavius* names a minor *Latin* poet whom *Horace* and *Virgil* ſatirized, conſequently a Poetaſter. The *Thames*, the *Cam*, and the *Iſis* (as the *Thames River* was frequently call'd at and above *Oxford*) ſhow that BUCKSKIN had ſtudied at *London*, *Cambridge*, and *Oxford*, tho' he had now emigrated to *America* (th' *Heſperian* Land). *Bœotia*, a Section of ancient *Greece*, was noted for the Stupidity of its Inhabitants, as was *Batavia (Holland)* in the Eighteenth Century.

Among thoſe whom *Burke* admir'd, *Richard* BLAND, a prominent Figure in the political Life of *Virginia*, was later to be mention'd in another Poem ("Quatrain"). So was *Richard Henry* LEE (see "An Epiſtle"), tho' in a leſs flattering Statement. In 1776, *Robert* BOLLING was a *Burgeſs* from *Dinwiddie County*. *Robert Carter* NICHOLAS was Treaſurer of the *Colony*. Rev. *John* CAMM, Profeſſor of Divinity at the *College of William and Mary*, defended the Rights of the Clergy againſt the Government. The PROPHET, alſo known as the EASTERN BARD (not *Burke* this time), had written a "Prophecy" for *Rind's Gazette, Auguſt* 15, 1766.

FRAGMENT OF A SATIRIC POEM (page 36) is compounded of two torn Sheets in the *State Department of Archives and Hiſtory*. Since the Top of the firſt Page is number'd "7," the Poem was obviouſly quite long. Perhaps the two Sheets are Part of that Production by *Burke* which "*Crambe*" mention'd in *Rind's Virginia Gazette, March* 12, 1767: "a Manuſcript Edition of the Rhapſodies of the Eaſt," a Portion of which, according to "*Crambe*," appear'd in the *Gazette* on *January* 22.

The extant mangled, truncated Manuſcript makes all but impoſſible any accurate Identification of Burke's References. A Man nam'd *Southy Simpſon* ſerv'd *Burke's* home County of *Accomack* in the *Virginia Houſe of Burgeſſes* during the mid 1760's. It can be eaſily believ'd that the peeviſh young *Iriſhman* found Fault with his local Repreſentative. The name *Noyon* has not been found in the Records of the Period. *Thomas Nelſon*, however, was already a Revolutionary Liberal in current Affairs. It is interefting to note that he and *Burke* later were together in the *Continental Congrefs*, and afterwards were *Governors* of adjoining States at the same Time.

The Signature MOROMASTIX ftands for *Scourge of Fools*. *The Country Planter* and Reverend *Cutler's The Scotch Rub* prefumably refer to popular Pieces from the Newfpapers, now buried in the ephemeral, perhaps loft, Prefs of the Day.

TRANSMOGRIFICATION (page 38) is from an untitled Manufcript in the *State Department of Archives and Hiftory*. Tho' there is no Evidence of its having appear'd in Print, this Poem is mention'd in an anonymous metrical Slander, "The Re-Metamorphofis of Landon Carter, Efq." (*Purdie's Virginia Gazette, June* 11, 1767), fign'd from *Norfolk, June* 1, 1767, which informs that there had been a Compofition in which

> . . . *gay Burke tells where*
> *Diana* bleffed him with a pair
>
> Of lufty ears . . . .

This *Gazette* Lampooner calls *Carter* "Litigious, haughty, headftrong"— as indeed the Son of *Robert "King" Carter* was. Wealthy, imperious, archly ariftocratic, and cauftic, *Landon Carter* was juft the Sort to fet off young democratic Blades like *Burke* into fcurrilous Iambics, which rather thunder'd perfonal Abufe than commented on the Iffues dividing them. *Carter's* "Clinks and Rhymes" have not been identified; but other Poems in the *Gazette* on *January* 1, 1767, and *Auguft* 13, 1767, mention *Carter* along with *Burke*.

In the Legend, the Hunter *Actæon* was turn'd into a Stag and kill'd by his own Dogs after *Cynthia* (*Diana*) caught him looking upon her at her Bath. *Cloacina* is *Venus* in her Role as *Goddefs of the Sewer*.

QUATRAIN (page 39), its four Lines untitled, is appended to the bottom of the Page on which *Burke* wrote his Poem "Tranfmogrification." *Richard Bland*, as a Refult of his Pamphlet "An Enquiry into the Rights of the Britifh Colonies" in 1766, was the Hero to all thofe in *Virginia* who oppof'd the *Stamp Act*. Evidently *Burke's* Elation is due to fome Recognition given him by *Bland*. The Lines are painfully youthful and egotiftical.

ON SEEING AN EXTRACT FROM THE BOSTON CHRONICLE (page 40) was evidently a lengthy Piece, judging from the Scrap of Manufcript in the *State Department of Archives and Hiftory*. Tho' the *Bofton Chronicle* was iffued only from 1767 to 1770, *Burke's* martial Lines, on the Bafis of his Handwriting as well as his Theme, were compof'd after the Beginning of the War.

COLIN AND CHLOË (page 41) appear'd in the *Gentleman's Magazine* (*London*) in 1778, the firft two Sections in *April*, the latter two in *May*. A Headnote explains that they were "Verfes written by Mr. Burke, a Delegate from North Carolina, and Mifs ———, of Philadelphia, June, 1777." Clearly, the literary Commerce between *London* and *Philadelphia* was not ferioufly hamper'd by the War.

The firſt three Sections, untitled, are fortunately preſerv'd in Manuſcript at the *State Department of Archives and Hiſtory*. Where the manuſcript Verſion differs from the printed one, the Manuſcript has been follow'd except in the Caſe of minor, obvious Errors.

Vaſtly different from *Burke's* maſculine Penmanſhip is the neat Script of *Chloë*. In the ſame Handwriting is a Letter to *Burke* dated *September* 13, 1777, and alſo preſerv'd in the *State Department of Archives and Hiſtory*. It is from a certain "N——— E———," who is writing to her *Colin*.

A third Manuſcript in the *Archives* is a ten-ſtanza Poem in *Burke's* undecipher'd Shorthand with this Meſſage on the Outſide: "Mr. Burke preſents his Compliments to Miſs Emlin, begs her to Accept of the Incloſed Appology for his not Obeying her Commands. He pretends not to merit the ſavor of Seeing Some of her Poetic reveries, but hopes it from her Gentleneſs and Generoſity."

Beyond this, nothing is known of the *Chloë* who was in reality *Miſs N. Emlin*. In the Intereſt of Totality, her two poetic Meſſages to *Burke* have been printed in Italics along with his own Compoſitions.

In her firſt Reply, *Chloë* cites the Patriot *Thomas Paine*. A *peaceful Land* may be underſtood by her Reference to *Shiloh*, a Meeting Place for the various Tribes of *Iſrael* during the Period of the *Judges*.

❦ ❦ ❦

RUTHLESS WAR (page 47) is untitled in the Manuſcript in the *State Department of Archives and Hiſtory*. The repeated Phraſes in the Poem, in addition to a Number of Corrections in *Burke's* careful Penmanſhip, indicate that this Verſion was not the final one ſent to *Chloë*.

This, the laſt of the *Colin-Chloë* Series, can be dated with ſome Accuracy. In her Letter of *September* 13, 1777, *Miſs N. Emlin* wrote *Burke* her Praiſe of "his deſcription of her Countries Woes" (*cf.* ſecond Stanza); conſequently, the Poem was written before that Date. It was two Days before, on *September* 11, that *Burke*, having forſaken temporarily the Halls of the *Continental Congreſs*, had fought in the Field near *Philadelphia* at the *Battle of Brandywine*. His agitated State of Mind at the Time of the approaching Encounter, and his Reaſons for daſhing off to the bloody Struggle againſt the *Britiſh*, are emotionally explor'd in the defiant Stanzas penn'd on the Eve of the Conflict.

❦ ❦ ❦

AN EPISTLE (page 50) appear'd unſign'd in the *Pennſylvania Evening Poſt* (*Philadelphia*), *July* 16, 1779. Four Names, their middle Letters miſſing (*e.g.*, P———a for *Paca*), have been ſpell'd out in the preſent Reprinting. A badly garbled Verſion of the Original appear'd in *William Boylan's Minerva* (*Raleigh*), *September* 19, 1803, naming *Burke* as the Author. *Boylan* credited *Relt's Pennſylvania Gazette* for an Opinion that the Poem was "a ſpecimen of luxuriant compoſition, as well as a forcible delineation of Paine's character" at that Time and later.

The Background of *Burke's* Attack on *Thomas Paine* was the famous *Silas Deane Affair*, which ſtirr'd the Members of the *Continental Congreſs* to ſuch violent Accuſations and Counteraccuſations that Sides were drawn as never before. In 1778, *Deane*, *Benjamin Franklin*, and *Arthur Lee* were diplomatic and economic Repreſentatives of the *Colonies* in *France*. Tho' *Franklin* was generally ſpar'd Cenſure for certain unexplain'd Matters in the Purchaſe of Supplies from *French*

Merchants, *Deane* and *Lee* were not. When *Deane* was recall'd to *Philadelphia* to account for his Actions, he accuf'd *Lee*, who had fpent much Time in *England* and had ftudied Medicine at *Edinburgh*, of being too amicable with the *Britifh* and therefore untruftworthy. Friends and Relatives of the *Virginian* rofe to his Defenfe.

In December, *Paine*, who had been appointed Secretary of the Foreign Affairs Committee as a Reward for ftirring Pamphlets of his like *Common Senfe*, ftepp'd into the Controverfy with a Stricture of *Deane* for his Remarks about *Lee*. He further was incenf'd that *France*, even while giving fecret Aid to the *Colonies*, was overtly at Peace with *England*. *Paine's* publifh'd Reports of *French* Aid were not only confider'd indifcrete coming from one in his official Capacity; he was, as *Burke* writes in his Poem, thought to be guilty of creating *Faction* at a Time when clof'd Ranks were of utmoft Importance. Members of the *Continental Congrefs* generally condemn'd his Interference, and on *January* 9, 1779, *Paine* submitted his Refignation. *Burke* was among thofe on *January* 16 who voted to accept it.

A Sidelight of all this was the *Berkenhout* Incident. *Dr. John Berkenhout*, a fellow Student of *Arthur Lee* at *Edinburgh*, arriv'd fufpicioufly in *America* in 1778 and fought patronage of *Arthur's* Brother *Richard Henry Lee*. Tho' *Berkenhout* was jail'd as a poffible Spy, he was later releaf'd for lack of Evidence. At any rate, the queftionable Relationfhip of *Arthur Lee* and the *Englifhman* caus'd additional Diftruft of the *American*, who was vigoroufly defended in many Letters by *Samuel Adams*, Member of *Congrefs* from *Maffachufetts*. The Cafe was more than em- barraffing to *Richard Henry Lee*, torn between the Need of explaining his Brother's Friendfhip and the Need to keep his Reputation for unequivocable Loyalty to the *Colonies* above Sufpicion. *Burke* had a low Opinion of the unrefolv'd Dilemma of *Richard Henry Lee*, already his Opponent in Congrefs over States' Rights. In earlier Years (*cf.* "Addrefs to the Goddefs Dulnefs"), *Burke* had greatly admir'd him.

Meanwhile *Paine*, with typical Energy, refuf'd to be filent on the *Affair*, preff'd his Arguments againft *Deane* and the *French* Alliance even after his Refignation, and criticiz'd the Actions of the *Congrefs*. Tho' *Burke* was only a mild Supporter of *Deane*, the *Faction*-creating *Paine* was downright obnoxious to him. *Paine*, in a Letter to *John Jay* as President of the *Congrefs* dated *March* 30, 1779, and a few Weeks later printed in the *Pennfylvania Packet* of *April* 20, nam'd eleven *Congrefs- men* who, *Paine* said, prevented Information on *Deane's* Double-Dealing from coming to Light. Among them, befides *Jay* and *Burke*, were *Gouverneur Morris* from *New York*, *William Paca* from *Maryland*, and *William Henry Drayton* of *South Carolina*. *Burke's* Poem fhows his Refentment of *Paine's* Faultfinding with thefe Men, and adds the Name of *James Duane* of *New York*, evidently an Object of *Paine's* Attack elfewhere.

In the beft Traditions of Eighteenth-Century Invective are *Burke's* Defenfe of his Friends, his invoking *Satan* and *Satan's* Daughter *Faction*, and his devaftating Description of *Paine's* anal Birth from *Pluto*.

TO MRS. VINING ON HIS DEPARTURE FROM PHILADELPHIA, AUGUST, 1779 (page 52) appears in the *State Records of North Carolina*, XV, 744. Wherein the printed Words depart from the Manufcript of this Poem in the *Southern Hiftorical Collection*, the Manufcript has been follow'd.

From *December* 14, 1778, to *Auguft* 14, 1779, *Burke* was in conftant Attendance at the *Continental Congrefs*. *Mrs. Efther Vining* and her Daughter liv'd at the *Philadelphia* Rooming Houfe where prominent *North Carolinians* habitually ftay'd. When *Burke* return'd to *Congrefs* the following Year, *Cornelius Harnett* wrote him from *Wilmington* on *April* 25: "I beg you will prefent mine & Mrs. *Harnett*'s very refpectful Compliments to Mrs. Burke, Mrs. & Mifs Vining, Mrs. Morrice, Mrs. Peters, & every other of my acquaintances."

LOVE OF GLORY (page 53) is untitled in the corrected Manufcript at the *State Department of Archives and Hiftory*, which alfo preferves an earlier, flightly different, incomplete Verfion. In one of the Manufcripts of the Poem, the Hero's Name is blank'd between the "M" and the "d"; in the other, a fecond Letter "a" is added. Neither is neceffary for Concealment, fince the full Name is later fpell'd out.

Lieutenant Colonel John Maitland, the *Britifh* officer who died in 1780 and was Subject of an Elegy by the "fair D——y," was much admir'd by all his *American* foes. Accounts proclaim him a verfatile and able Officer. After outftanding Service in *South Carolina*, he led his Troops thro' the Swamps to reinforce *General Prévoft* during the Siege of *Savannah*. *Burke*'s Lines had fpecial Reference to *Maitland*'s building of Redoubts at *Savannah* and the indecifive Maneuvers which took place near them. Certainly the Poet was willing to admit the Virtues of an Opponent, particularly the flain Warrior of the fair Elegift, tho' unwilling to let the Occafion pafs without an equally good Word for the courageous *Americans*.

A NEW SONG (page 54), fo titled in the Manufcript in the *State Department of Archives and Hiftory*, is a Prothalamion to the "fair D——y" of *Burke*'s "Love of Glory." He left no Clue to help identify the Lady or her Hufband, who is given the paftoral Name *Strephon*. Among his Papers in the *Archives*, however, are three Stanzas in neat Script titled "In Anfwer to a Compliment in Verfe," a Reply from "D——y" to *Burke*'s two Poems:

> *"That Fair" accepts the compliment*
> *As witty as polite;*
> *Hers, in return, as well is meant*
> *Tho' fhe, like B——, can't write.*
>
> *When candid he commends his Foe,*
> *Tells how in Arms they've fhone,*
> *And ftrives their Fame & Worth to fhow,*
> *He plainly proves his own.*
>
> *Lefs candid may fhe never be,*
> *But free from Party Spirit,*
> *To real Virtue bend the Knee*
> *And yield the Palm to Merit.*

A LOCK OF DELIA'S HAIR (page 55) is tranſcrib'd from the untitled Manuſcript in the *State Department of Archives and Hiſtory*. The laſt twelve Lines ſhow Reviſions. Its late Compoſition is evinc'd in *Damon's* acknowledging that his Youth is paſt and his Hair is "ſilver." *Burke* left no Hint as to the Identity of *Delia*.

PENSIVE DELIA (page 56) is untitled in the Manuſcript in the *State Department of Archives and Hiſtory*.

TO UNRESPONSIVE DELIA (page 57), originally addreſſ'd to *"Maria,"* is match'd from two untitled manuſcript Fragments in the *State Department of Archives and Hiſtory*.

DAMON'S ADVICE TO HIMSELF (page 58) was written on the Back of a Letter informing one of *Burke's* military Correſpondents about the anticipated Movement of certain *Britiſh* Troops from *New York* and *Rhode Iſland* to the *South*. The untitled Manuſcript in the *State Department of Archives and Hiſtory* ſhows a Number of Corrections in *Burke's* Handwriting.

SONG FOR MISS GILCHRIST (page 59) was printed firſt in the *State Gazette of North Carolina (Edenton), July* 9, 1790; then G. J. McRee, in *Life and Correſpondence of James Iredell,* vol. I (1857), 563-564, reprinted it and added to whatever Errors the *State Gazette* had made. The *Gazette* gave it ſimply the Title "Song" and cautiouſly warn'd that it was "ſaid to have been compoſed by Thos. Burke, Eſq." The *Iredell* Book gave full Credit to *Burke* but claim'd that the Verſes, "preſerved by Judge Iredell," had never before been publiſh'd. For this preſent third Printing, the Manuſcript in the *Department of Archives and Hiſtory*, in *Burke's* unmiſtakable Handwriting, has been follow'd.

The most felicitous Phraſe in the Poem is unfortunately not of *Burke's* Inſpiration. Concerning *Cornwallis, Colonel Dudley* wrote to *Burke* on *September* 3, 1781, that it was his "flattering hope of having it in my power before many days to inform you of his being completely Burgoyned." Indeed, at *Yorktown* on *October* 19, 1781, *Cornwallis* was to be as hopeleſſly cloſ'd in as had the *Britiſh* Commander *Burgoyne* at *Saratoga* four Years earlier.

The *Miſs Gilchriſt* of the Title was probably one of the four Daughters of *Mrs. Martha Gilchriſt* of *Halifax*, where *Burke* had many Friends. *Mrs. Gilchriſt* was reputed to be "deſcended from and allied to ſome of the firſt families" of *North Carolina*. Since the Poem was written for a young Lady, *Burke's* Emphaſis is not on War, but on the Return to domeſtic Happineſs. In the laſt Stanza, he adviſes *Miſs Gilchriſt* and her Siſters as to their Duties when they become Mothers.